LARRY LARUE'S

Major League Encounters

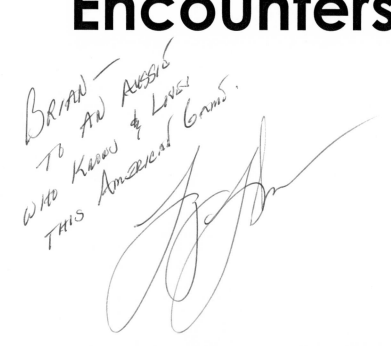

The Inside Story on the Funny, Tragic, Painful, Man-to-Man World of Major League Baseball

Larry LaRue
Author of Major League Encounters

 For more than 30 years sportswriter Larry LaRue of the Tacoma News Tribune has had a front-row seat to the unfolding drama and comedy of life among the people who make up baseball's major leagues. In this book, he shares his experiences and tells the stories of the people of baseball – their strengths, their weaknesses, their desires, their demons – and the game they all love.

LaRue has long roots as a writer. His grandmother was a typesetter – in the days when stories were cast in hot lead – for a weekly in San Dimas, Calif. He would sit on her lap as she ran the Linotype machine. He was first published at 10, when a San Clemente newspaper ran his story on Pookie, his dog. He began covering sports at the Antelope Valley News at 18 and became sports editor a year later.

Since those days, LaRue has worked for five newspapers, a business journal, and an entertainment magazine. He's also had brief careers as a window washer, a bouncer, and a private investigator.

Through it all, he wrote.

Major League Encounters is his first book.

Major League Encounters

One hundred personal stories of the select group of men who make their living playing a game

BY LARRY LARUE

ISBN-978-0-9837873-2-7

Reader Publishing Group
Long Beach CA 90802

Visit our website at www.readerpublishing.com

Printed in the United States of America

"For Marie and Jessica, who gave me the time to live amongst the diamonds and the clubhouses."

MAJOR LEAGUE ENCOUNTERS

1. Jim Abbott: Nothing Special About Him

2. Rich Amaral: He Never Gave Up

3. Ryan Anderson: Dominating At 17, Out By 25

4. Sparky Anderson: Always Loved The Game

5. Eric Anthony: Never Took A Day For Granted

6. Tim Belcher: Raging Intensity

7. David Bell: Baseball Was A Family Affair

8. Adrian Beltre: A Balls-Out Player

9. Juan Beniquez: The Fearful Flyer

10. Yuniesky Betancourt: Nice Guy Who Fell Short

11. Willie Bloomquist: Pushed By Dad To Be His Best

12. Mike Blowers: Lived The Game On Field and Off

13. Bert Blyleven: A Burning Desire

14. Barry Bonds: Don't Take Him Personally

15. Bob Boone: A Know-It-All Who Knew It All

16. Bret Boone: Call Him 'The Boone'

17. Chris Bosio: Speed Is Not The Answer

18. Jim Bouton: He Changed The Game's Image

19. Larry Bowa: Not So Nice, But Not So Bad Either

20. Milton Bradley: At War With His Demons

21. Darren Bragg: Roses And Remembrance

22. Bill Buckner: An Error, Closure And Forgiveness

23. Jay Buhner: The Buzzcut King

24. Ken Caminiti: Didn't Mind Getting Dirty

25. Rod Carew: Not One To Suffer In Silence

26. Norm Charlton: Old School Tough

27. Jeff Cirillo: Too Sensitive For Tough Love

28. Ken Cloude: Playing With Guilt

29. Ben Davis: Looking Good Was Not Enough

30. Tim Davis: Putting Big Payday In Perspective

31. Brian Downing: Didn't Make High School Team

32. Dennis Eckersley: Passion And Precision

33. Cecil Fielder: It's Hard For A Big Man To Steal

34. Doug Fister: Overlooked Talent

35. Jim Fregosi: He Took It All Personally

36. Freddy Garcia: Living Large And Playing Hard

37. Kirk Gibson: If You're Not Here To Win, Then Why?

38. Charles Gipson: He Crossed The Union Line

39. Dwight Gooden: One Last Chance At Glory

40. Rich Gossage: An Intimidating Presence

41. Ken Griffey Sr: Quick To Anger

42. Ken Griffey Jr.: Couldn't Forgive A Slight

43. Vladimir Guerrero: High Or Low, He Hit Them All

44. Tony Gwynn: A Heavy-Weight At Bat

45. Bill Haselman: Beaned By A Girl

46. Sterling Hitchcock: Keeping It Real

47. Frank Howard: He Called And Everyone Came

48. Brian Hunter: Owed His Speed To His Sister

49. Butch Huskey: Not Too Big for the Big League

50. Ichiro: Zen Meets Baseball

51. Bo Jackson: In An Elite World, He Was Special

52. Reggie Jackson: Ego And Magic

53. Bruce Kison: Nobody Wanted On His Hit Parade

54. Bobby Knoop: It Wasn't His Glove Or His Bat

55. Casey Kotchman: Not A Smiley Guy

56. Tony LaRussa: Willing To Share His Wisdom

57. Fred Lynn: Does Playing Hurt, Hurt the Team?

58. John Mabry: Keeping It In Perspective

59. Josias Manzanillo: Line Drive Puts Him Down

60. Edgar Martinez: He Never Forgot Who He Was

61. Tino Martinez: The Best Revenge

62. Don Mattingly: Last Game Was His Best

63. Gene Mauch: He Managed The Way He Played

64. Willie Mays: A Talk In The Park

65. Jack McKeon: Old Man In Young Man's Game

66. Kevin Mitchell: Hard To Stay Out Of Trouble

67. Paul Molitor: He Did What He Had To Do

68. Mike Morse: Clueless In Seattle

69. Jamie Moyer: Never Say It's Over Until It's Over

70. Tony Muser: A Fire Ball Couldn't Stop Him

71. Jeff Nelson: Surrounded By Girls

72. John Olerud: A Man Of Few Words

73. Jim Palmer: Baseball Legend with A Gift For Gab

74. Tony Phillips: A Short Man With A Big Chip

75. Lou Piniella: Tough Guy With A Soft Heart

76. Bryan Price: When Failure Comes Knocking

77. Kirby Puckett: From The Projects To Hall of Fame

78. J.J. Putz: Merry Prankster With A Subtle Touch

79. Harold Reynolds: Always Ready To Talk Baseball

80. Cal Ripken Jr: Just Get The Job Done

81. Alex Rodriguez: Tightly Controlled Image

82. Nolan Ryan: He Demanded Respect, Or Else …

83. Ryne Sandberg: Just Wanted To Play The Game

84. Jeff Schaefer: Haunted By Anger At His Father

85. David Segui: Sense Of Fun Not Always Shared

86. Carlos Silva: Stirring The Poo

87. Jim Slaton: Loved The Game, Loved His Brother

88. Luis Sojo: Always A Major Leaguer

89. Sammy Sosa: From Shoe Factory To Sports Hero

90. Bill Swift: Born To Be A Baseball Player

91. Frank Thomas: They Called Him 'The Big Hurt'

92. Andre Thornton: From Tragedy To Triumph

93. Steve Trout: Not Mystical, Just Sensitive

94. Mo Vaughn: Not A Fan Of The Press

95. Omar Vizquel: Gentle Man With G-Rated Humor

96. Larry Walker: OCD For The Number Three

97. Tom Wilhelmsen: Baseball Or Dope? Baseball

98. Dick Williams: Hated Writers, But Needed Them

99. Dan Wilson: Didn't Like To Talk About Himself

100. Tiger Woods: Dropping By For Batting Practice

Introduction

Millions of us grow up wanting to play in the big leagues and each season 750 men do.

Thirty teams, 25 players each. It's an exclusive club. There are a few more on the disabled list, but they're never really certain the job they had when they were first injured will be open when they return.

It's the nature of the major league game. For every player who is put on a roster, another is removed. We tend to look at the exceptions, like Jamie Moyer, and think all careers last decades.

Most last less than three years.

The minute I began covering the game late in the summer of 1979, people began asking me for stories about the players.

My father loved hearing them. My friends would ask what Reggie Jackson was really like, what talking to Willie Mays was like. A few years ago, I began writing down the tales of the men I'd covered, planning to give them to my daughter. That's how this book began, although it wasn't a book at the time.

As the collection of stories grew, I realized again how unique are the men who play major league baseball. They aren't young gods of sport; they are men with either great physical gifts or enormous drive – and sometimes both.

And still, it isn't always enough.

Major league baseball devours great players and breaks hearts not just every spring, but almost every day of the year. They've all grown up being the best on their teams, and most have never failed at anything – at least not on the field.

But at the big league level, they encounter obstacles that never existed for them elsewhere. Relentless travel and a 162-game season wear their bodies down.

Early in their careers, they don't play regularly, and sometimes they platoon with another player – something they've never been asked to do before.

Balls that were hits at every other level are outs in the majors, where defenders routinely steal them.

I remember when the Seattle Mariners drafted Jeff Clement in the first round, and after proper minor league seasoning he was brought up. One of the first pitchers he faced was then-Toronto ace Roy Halladay.

Not only did Halladay dominate Seattle that night, he threw pitches that Clement – a catcher – had never seen before.

"I don't even know what those pitches were," Clement told me afterward.

That's the size of the transition.

And every first-time, big league player suffers that transition. The truth is, most don't adjust. When there are 40,000 fans in the park, when the manager is glaring and teammates are counting on them, pitchers often lose the strike zone and hitters expand it by wildly chasing anything airborne.

After the Mariners had blown through a half-dozen rookie pitchers one season, I asked manager Lou Piniella if he thought he was hard on young pitchers.

"Not as hard as they are on me," he said.

Which makes every one of those 750 major league players

a special case. They are judged almost daily on how well they play, and they all know that every team has the depth to explore options.

You're slumping? There's a kid in Class AAA that's tearing it up and looks ready. Had a tough run out of the bullpen? There's always a young arm – or a veteran hoping for another shot – waiting somewhere.

What I enjoyed as much as anything I saw on the field, were the moments before and after games, talking to the players, coaches and managers.

A common denominator?

Only one. Each of them had been enchanted by baseball as kids. Managers in their 60s and players in their 30s – they're all in love with a game that lets them put on a uniform each day and play.

It cost many their wives and created thousands of kids who saw more of their dads on television than they did at home. Many players are good enough to stay in the game for years – just not with the same team. So they move, sometimes two or three times in a season. But none of that matters. They still love baseball.

The money helps. The major league minimum salary is close to $450,000. The average is skewed by players such as Alex Rodriguez, who signed a $275 million, over-10-year contract with the New York Yankees.

Still, to a man, they played the game for far less – often for nothing – before getting to the majors. Most minor league players have off-season jobs.

When baseball struck in 1981, one of the Angels outfielders, Larry Harlow, had to work construction with a friend to make ends meet. The difference between staying on a big league roster or being sent out to the minors can force players in their mid to late-20s out of the sport.

They can't support a family on a minor league salary.

And still, walking away from baseball is the most difficult decision most players will have made in their lives.

Late in his career, I asked Reggie Jackson if he could picture his final day in uniform.

"No," he said. "And I know it's coming."

There may be no place in the world quite like a big league clubhouse, and every retired player – or beat writer – I know admits they miss that atmosphere as much as the game itself.

In the clubhouse, men under pressure become child-like again.

I remember Bret Boone running through the clubhouse wearing nothing but motorcycle chaps one day. Jay Buhner outdid him. Jay ran screaming from the clubhouse to the training room one morning wearing only a bagel.

When he returned to his locker he pulled the bagel off and took a bite. Ken Griffey Jr. laughed so hard, he fell off his stool.

Outrageous dares, kangaroo courts, mock rages and occasionally real ones, none of it scripted.

Non-players entered at their own risk. I've seen a player give complete interviews to television crews who believed he was someone else, all the time puzzled by his bizarre answers.

Yes, Virginia, players love fun. At anyone's expense.

In Kansas City, the Royals had a camera crew on the field before each series, freshening up mug shots of players for their enormous outfield scoreboard.

A photo crew mistook Seattle reserve infielder Jeff Schaefer for outfielder Dave Cochrane one afternoon, and Schaeffer happily posed for the crew – the bill of his cap turned up, his dark glasses askew, and a very strange smile on his face.

No matter how many retakes the crew asked for, they got the same look.

That night, when Cochrane first came to the plate, the Royals scoreboard showed an enormous picture of Schaefer. Players in the Mariners dugouts were in hysterics.

Even Cochrane, bat in hand at the plate, had to back away for a moment.

In the 32 years I've covered major league baseball, I've dealt with more than a few thousand players, coaches and managers. I began with the belief that none of them owed me their time, so I always asked for it.

Over the years, players have said things to me in anger, in frustration, and as long as we were talking one-on-one, I would ask them afterward if they were sure that's what they wanted to say.

I wasn't trying to change their story. I certainly wasn't averse to a scoop.

But knowing a player well, I could tell when what he was saying was totally out of character. Twice, I told a player I was going to hold the quote overnight and ask again the next day.

Covering big league baseball is a long-term proposition. My theory was not to burn a player who clearly was speaking emotionally, especially if he was talking only to me.

Clubhouse outbursts? Once they were seen, they were fair game.

To cover a beat well, however, you have to build relationships, not just write stories. Publishing a foolish quote that's apologized for the next day may get you higher placement for the day, but it burns that player – and likely others – as viable interviews for years.

That didn't mean I covered for players or teams. When Milton Bradley or Ichiro or Randy Johnson said something outrageous, not in the heat of the moment but as a statement of belief, I wrote it.

When the best player I ever covered, Ken Griffey Jr., had lost so much interest in games he wasn't playing, he began napping in the clubhouse, I verified it and wrote it.

It ended a 20-year relationship I considered my favorite in the game.

The stories included here aren't meant to be full biographies, just moments, encounters, with a cross-section of major league players. Some went to the Hall of Fame. Others barely cracked the lineup with any regularity.

All of them let me into their worlds, and I've found their candor, humor and humanity worth writing about for more than half my life. They weren't all great players. They weren't all great men.

On any given day, however, they are one of only 750 men in the world to play big league baseball.

And that alone made them special.

– Larry LaRue

Jim Abbott: Nothing Special About Him

It was the spring of 1989, and the then-California Angels had signed and brought to camp an Olympic hero – the pitcher who'd won the Gold Medal game for the U.S. – and the hottest interview in sports.

Jim Abbott was 21 and bright, driven and thoughtful. So were most big league rookies.

What made Abbott an athlete pursued by everything from the Today Show to the New York Times before he'd thrown a major league pitch?

Abbott had only one hand.

In his first 10 days in camp, the Angels received 120 interview requests, including mine. I was penciled in the first day Abbott faced a big league hitter – teammate Lance Parrish – in batting practice.

I asked Abbott how long it took most interviewers to get to the birth defect that left him without a right hand.

"All of them kind of start differently," he said. "Usually about the third or fourth question, though, they get around to asking, 'What's it like to be a one-handed pitcher?'"

His answer never varied.

"I guess it's like being a two-handed pitcher. I've been doing things the same way since I was a child," Abbott said.

Three hundred-game winner Don Sutton talked at length to Abbott after Abbott had signed his first professional contract. The topic was interviews and autographs.

"Don told me 'It's the rent you pay for that wonderful space you occupy,'" Abbott said.

Of course, Abbott's story was already viewed as an inspiration to children everywhere with birth defects – something he'd been aware of for years.

"Maybe some young girl or boy will read something and think, 'If Jim Abbott can do it, so can I,' and that would be great," Abbott said.

"But that's not why I play baseball."

Abbott had turned down movie offers and book deals. Getting this far, his first spring training in the big leagues, wasn't where he wanted his story to end.

"Sometimes I get a little frustrated with all this attention and I want to scream, 'Hey, I can play baseball – this other thing doesn't matter,'" Abbott said. "They all focus on my missing hand. So maybe the only way to prove it is to just keep going.

"Maybe the majors is the only place I can prove that."

Abbott had been proving himself since Little League, when his parents worried he would be hurt by not being able to field his position. It was never a factor.

When he gripped the baseball in his left hand, he'd balance his fielding glove on his right forearm. In one quick, practiced move, after he delivered the pitch, he would slip the glove onto his left hand and field the ball.

Then, with another slight-of-hand, he'd transfer the glove back to his right forearm, grab the ball with his left hand and throw the runner out.

"All my life, I've loved baseball and played it at every level I could," he said. "Now, I'm playing here, against the best in the world.

"Always before, my best has been good enough. All I ever wanted was to find out if my best was good enough at this level. People write what they want. But for me, that's why I'm playing."

Like so many folks that spring, I found Abbott fascinating – a kid who didn't consider himself special, though he'd never failed in any athletic endeavor.

He'd been a high school quarterback, the ace of the Michigan Big-Ten team, a Gold Medalist. The fact that he had done it all with one hand seemed to impress everyone but Abbott.

Jim Abbott made the team that first spring and never spent a day in the minor leagues. He pitched for 10 seasons in the majors, threw a no-hitter for the New York Yankees, won 87 games.

I talked to him again late in his career, when he'd started five games for the Chicago White Sox and won each of them.

"When I lost games last year – and I lost a lot of them – people wrote that I was washed up," Abbott told me. "I thought it was kind of cool that they didn't say I was a washed up one-handed pitcher."

It was, perhaps, the ultimate achievement of Abbott's career that he made teammates, opponents, fans and the media forget that.

Rich Amaral: He Never Gave Up

For nine years, Rich Amaral did time in the minor leagues, and for eight of them his cellmate was his wife, Michele.

A phenom out of UCLA, a kid with a business degree and a real estate license, Amaral kept chasing baseball long after it stopped chasing him.

The year he turned 27, he was the oldest prospect on the Chicago White Sox Class AA team. A year later, he was the oldest player in the White Sox farm system.

"I played in every ballpark in America," Amaral told me, "except those in the American and National League."

And every step of the way, Michele went with him.

"I loved the game and I loved Rich," she said. "Everywhere we went, we found something to enjoy. We froze in Massachusetts and Vancouver, and it got awfully hot in Birmingham, but there were wonderful people and good times."

Seven years into his professional career, Amaral qualified for federal aid. He didn't take it, but he also never seriously considered doing anything besides play baseball for a living.

"I just tried to get better," Amaral said. "I was in AA ball four years in a row."

Amaral's first-year roommate – before marrying Michele – was a future teammate on the Seattle Mariners, Jamie Moyer.

"He was a surfer then, and he'd always greet everyone the same way, 'Hey, dude!'" Moyer said of Amaral. "I remember a lot of nights sitting in our apartment talking about why the organization called up this guy or that one.

"He hasn't changed that much. He wasn't married then, but he was dating Michele, so they were a couple," Moyer said.

Amaral had trouble explaining to non-baseball friends how he could have a real estate license yet live close to the poverty line on minor league salaries year after year.

"Michele packed and moved so many times she started thinking it was normal," he said. "When my son was 15 months old, he'd been to more places than most adults."

When he was finally called to the big leagues, it was because Seattle shortstop Omar Vizquel got hurt – and Amaral could play shortstop, second base, first base, and the outfield.

A line-drive hitter with speed, Amaral flourished playing on the Kingdome's artificial turf, and after small opportunities in 1991 and 1992, he got the chance to play 110 games for the Mariners in '93.

Why? Lou Piniella.

A grizzled bear of a manager, Piniella didn't have many weapons his first year in Seattle, but he saw one he liked in Amaral that first spring.

"He can play anywhere, he can run, he can hit a little bit, and I like him," Piniella said. "The question I asked him was 'Where the hell have you been?'"

The answer: Almost everywhere.

That season, under Piniella, Amaral batted .290 in the first extended major league play of his career.

He was 31-years-old.

Meanwhile, Moyer joined the team as a journeyman left-handed pitcher, one Piniella put in his starting rotation and told to be ready every fifth day. Across the clubhouse, Moyer admitted, he and Amaral would make eye contact and smile.

"It's a long way and a lot of years since Winston-Salem," Moyer said.

"Back then, the team travelled in a bus that always broke down. At home, Richie would try to sleep in and the landlord was always on him because he put tin foil in the bedroom windows."

Amaral remembered facing Moyer in a spring training exhibition game one year.

"I doubled, and he turned around on the mound and yelled at me, 'Hey! I'm trying to make this team," Amaral said. "And I yelled back, "I'm trying to make this team, too.'

"We made it because we were willing to stay with it, work hard and never give up. I remember Michele and me living in a rented room with about two feet on either side of the bed – and it wasn't a big bed."

In the end, Amaral played all or parts of 10 major league seasons. He and Michele are still happily married room-mates.

Ryan Anderson: Dominating At 17, Out By 25

He was considered an athlete by age 5, and at 15 he could throw a baseball as hard as any Michigan high school pitcher ever had. So it's not surprising that Ryan Anderson expected to conquer major league baseball.

The Seattle Mariners made him the 19th player picked in the 1997 June draft. In his first press conference, Anderson was asked what his goals were.

"I want to be one of the best pitchers who ever pitched," he said.

It wasn't false bravado. Anderson was still 17 and had no reason to believe he wouldn't dominate. A 6-foot-10 left-hander, he'd never found hitters all that challenging, or pitching all that difficult.

But, Anderson didn't get it. At his age, not many do. He'd always been the best player, and hadn't learned yet that in professional baseball everyone had been the best player somewhere.

When he threw his first round of batting practice in the spring of '98, he faced three of the better hitters in Seattle history – Ken Griffey Jr., Edgar Martinez and Jay Buhner. No matter that it was the first day of full workouts for batters, Anderson was sky high.

Unfortunately, he shared his excitement with the media.

"I completely dominated them," Anderson said afterward.

By the time he got to the clubhouse the next day,

Anderson's locker had been rearranged. That quote was pasted to one wall, and veterans came by facetiously asking for his autograph.

It was a career of hard lessons and bad luck for Anderson.

Anderson's father didn't help matters, though he tried. After learning that his son would face Oakland in a spring game, Gus went to the Athletics camp a day earlier and tried to videotape hitters.

He was escorted out of camp – a story that made the papers and again embarrassed Anderson.

Still, three seasons into a minor league career, the kid had gone from Class A to Class AAA and was on the verge of making the Mariners in the spring of '01.

Then his rotator cuff went, and he missed a full season. A year later, it was his labrum. In 2003, a second tear in the labrum. Another surgery, another missed season.

The injuries were devastating, more so because Anderson's efforts to come back from them were viewed by those in the Seattle organization as less than extraordinary. He did what he was told to do and went on about his life, expecting that marvelous left arm to rebound.

It never did.

Before he turned 25, Anderson was out of baseball. Asked what he planned to do, it turned out his confidence hadn't failed him. Anderson said he thought he might play professional basketball.

Anderson became a chef.

Sparky Anderson: Always Loved the Game

In the summer of '93, the Detroit Tigers thought they could contend, and manager Sparky Anderson managed accordingly. During a three-game series in Seattle, he ordered his pitchers to walk Ken Griffey Jr. seven times.

Late in the final game of that series, Griffey homered – and when he reached home plate, looked directly into the Detroit dugout and grabbed his crotch.

Anderson laughed.

"Junior was reacting to the seven walks," the manager said. "If I was that kind of player and I was walked all those times with all those men on base – knowing the damage I could do – I'd be angry, too."

Would he have grabbed his crotch?

"Probably not," Anderson said, smiling.

Sparky Anderson was a class act from his days managing Cincinnati's 'Big Red Machine' to his pushing the Tigers to a World Series. And when his team got bad, Anderson remained one of baseball's grand ambassadors.

By '95, Sparky was 61-years-old and in his final year in the majors.

The first few weeks of that season, he brought Detroit back into Seattle, and this time he knew the Tigers weren't going to contend. He knew, too, that he was close to the end of a superb managerial career.

"I'm dried up old leather," he said, sitting in the Kingdome. "I remember Ken Griffey Jr. and the other kids sitting in my office drinking soda pop."

The game has changed from those more innocent times.

"Fans have gotten into the show business aspect of baseball. It used to be if they came to the park and saw a good game, they went home happy." Anderson said.

"Now, that's not enough. They want to see their favorite celebrity do well, too."

Anderson watched Griffey signing autographs.

"If fans are wearing his shoes, his cap, his jackets, they want to see him succeed," Anderson said. "My job as manager is to take the best player in baseball out of the game if I can. If you pitch to him, he's going to show you why he's the best player in the game."

Later that night, Griffey came to the plate in a crucial late-inning situation, with two men on base and Jay Buhner on deck. Right-hander Sean Bergman was pitching, and Anderson went to the mound.

He had a left-hander warming in the bullpen. He also had 34,000 fans in the Kingdome screaming not to walk Griffey.

Bergman stayed in the game and pitched to Griffey. Junior homered to win the game.

Poor managing?

Anderson certainly could have been excused for walking Griffey intentionally and facing Buhner with the bases loaded. That was the by-the-book decision.

But it was April, and neither the Tigers nor the Mariners were going anywhere. Bergman had already retired Griffey twice.

As importantly, Anderson knew how much baseball in Seattle had struggled, how much a big crowd like that one meant to the Mariners.

Anderson gave that crowd what it wanted – an at-bat, not

an intentional walk.

"I don't always claim to be right," Anderson said afterward, "but I've always done what I felt I had to do. Maybe my time has come and gone, but I have always loved this game."

Eric Anthony: Never Took A Day For Granted

Eric Anthony played the game hard, and enjoyed the clubhouse. But he never had trouble leaving the ballpark behind him.

Life had taught him hard lessons before he got to the majors – he'd worked a few minimum wage jobs, then watched an older brother wither away and die of AIDs. He cared about baseball but never took himself or anyone else too seriously.

One day in 1994, a reporter got a tip from the U.S. Postal Service – one of their drug-sniffing dogs had seized a package addressed to Anthony, care of the Seattle Mariners.

Anthony's response?

"They'd better get a new dog," he said.

When postal authorities got his permission to open the box in question, it contained two new baseball caps – sent to Anthony from an inner-city baseball program in Los Angeles he had supported financially.

The post office didn't retire the dog, nor did it apologize for the leak implying Anthony may have been involved in some drug scheme. And it never released the caps to Anthony, insisting they were evidence.

If Anthony never had the career some scouts projected, he still played nine years in the majors. He never took a day or a friend for granted, and he tried to live life for a brother whose time was too short.

Tim Belcher: Raging Intensity

Tim Belcher played the game with intensity that often slid into full rage. It was that temperament that allowed him to leave a lasting mark on the game.

That mark was right there in the bowels of old Yankee Stadium, and it stayed there until the park was demolished.

"Belcher's Line," as it came to be known, was painted on the floor of the hallway outside the visiting clubhouse – a bright red barrier to the media placed about 40 feet from the clubhouse door – after the night of Oct. 4, 1995.

That was the night the Mariners and Yankees played a 15-inning Game 2 in the American League Division Series that was decided on a last-pitch home run by New York's Jim Leyritz. The man who threw that pitch was Belcher.

As he battled his emotions coming off the mound, through the dugout and up the tunnel toward the clubhouse, Belcher could think only that he'd put his team in an 0-2 hole in the series, that he'd thrown the wrong pitch and lost the most important game of his career.

As he turned the corner toward the clubhouse, there was a television camera – literally in his face – and a man with a microphone asking how it felt to end the game in such a dramatic fashion.

Belcher exploded, pushing the camera away from him and raging into the clubhouse. The network cried foul. The players demanded a cooling off period. The next day, the league rules changed. Camera crews had to wait beyond the "Belcher Line," along with the rest of the media, until the clubhouse opened.

Belcher had single-handedly ended "ambush journalism" in baseball.

A hot-headed farm boy early in his career, Belcher grew to be a studious, thoughtful man, on and off the mound. Much of his anger was aimed squarely at himself, and though he never quite learned to control all of that, he was never beyond making light of it.

Talking to Belcher about his anger, he said he'd managed over the years to vent it and let it go, and tried never to let it interfere with the lives and jobs of others.

"I'll never leave you without a story," he told me. "That wouldn't be fair."

One night in Kansas City, Belcher pitched poorly and, not for the first time in his career, was ejected for arguing with umpires. After the game, the press descended upon Belcher's locker, only to find he'd long since departed.

That wasn't unprecedented. Many players took bad games home early. Belcher, however, was too professional to leave the media with nothing – and he was good to his word never to leave me without a story.

Taped to his cubicle was a Q & A, with Belcher having supplied both the questions and the answers – and nailing the typical post-game questions perfectly.

Belcher had his demons throughout a career that produced 146 major league wins, but he never lost his perspective and never took his anger out on teammates or the media.

David Bell: Baseball Was A Family Affair

It was David Bell's decision, though he may never have had a choice.

The son of one major league player, the grandson of another, baseball was more than a family tradition. It was what the Bell men did.

"It was like a link for all of us," Bell said. "I remember telling my father when I was about 5-years-old that I wanted to play baseball for a living. He could have laughed, but he didn't.

"He'd told his father the same thing when he was about the same age."

Baseball was the family business.

David's grandfather, Gus, played 15 years in the majors and batted .281 with 206 home runs. His father, Buddy, played 18 years in the big leagues and batted .279 with 201 home runs.

David Bell and his brothers Mike and Rick all played professionally.

During his time in Seattle, Bell blossomed as a player – something few people outside his immediate family were certain would ever happen.

"When I was drafted, I weighed about 155 pounds," Bell said. "I wasn't strong. I think my dad's career worked in my favor. Cleveland saw a little talent and projected I'd get stronger, based on my dad's career."

Early on, that projection wavered. When Bell struggled, though, he had the benefit of family counsel.

"I'd call my grandpa all the time, and he never said a negative thing to me, ever," Bell said. "He knew first-hand the game could be negative, he knew how hard it could be.

"Whether I had a good game or bad one, he'd always say something positive to me.

Gus Bell died in 1995, the year David played his first 41 games in the majors.

David's father, Buddy, had retired as a player in 1989, but the year after Bell made it to the big leagues, his father was named manager of the Detroit Tigers and would go on to manage three teams over a nine-year career.

I'd known Buddy as a player and manager, and when I talked to him one spring about David, he smiled and shook his head.

"Somewhere along the line, our relationship changed," he said. "I'm still his father, he's still my son, but he's one of my best friends. We talk about everything."

I asked Bell how often he talked to his father.

"We probably talk every day, most weeks," he said.

Buddy Bell said David played baseball without being a strong physical presence growing up, but that he never let his size factor into his game.

"He was tough, and he loved to compete," Buddy said. "At every level, he got the job done. He was skinny, small and he was never real strong growing up, but he always got the job done.

"You can scout a lot of things, but you can't measure toughness. David was tough then, he's tough now – and he still gets the job done."

David was a quiet man with the media, though when I asked about his father and grandfather, he was animated.

"I was always proud of my dad and my grandpa," he said. "Give them credit, they never pushed any of us into the game and once we all started playing as kids, they never put their expectations on us. I loved baseball, but I never felt pressured to play.

"I didn't want to disappoint them, but that was how I felt, not how they felt. They taught me a lot about life, not just baseball."

An example? David Bell was 26 when he arrived in Seattle, and had been traded four times.

"I never look back," he said. "My grandpa told me to always look to the future, stay positive and keep working. I never sit down when a season is over and think too much about it. I'm not like that."

Bell's career lasted 12 seasons, and he hit 123 home runs, batted .257, never said much but never burned a bridge. The Bell men became just the second family in baseball history to have three generations play in the majors. The other family was the Boones – Ray Boone, his son Bob, and his grandsons Bret and Aaron.

Not long after he retired as a player, David began managing in the minor leagues. The goal was to become a big league manager, like his father.

"I have a lot of pride in our family, and there's personal satisfaction in carrying on what my father and grandfather did. I'm part of them, just like my brothers and sisters are."

Adrian Beltre: A Balls Out Player

Adrian Beltre may be the best-fielding third baseman in the history of the game, and as we found out midway through his career, he had to be.

The man didn't wear a protective cup.

Weird moments surrounded his career, beginning from the time he signed a professional contract with the Los Angeles Dodgers – at age 15. That was a year too early, and the team was slapped with a considerable penalty by the commissioner for its action.

A loud, hilariously in-your-face teammate, Beltre would argue with anyone over anything. On the field, no one ever doubted his commitment.

They couldn't.

During the winter of 2001, Beltre was at home in the Dominican Republic when his appendix burst. An operation was botched and, two months later, he was in spring training with an infected, seeping surgery site.

Beltre played until the team said "no mas," then underwent a second abdominal surgery. A month later, he was back at third base.

After the best season of his career in 2004, when he batted .334 with 48 home runs and 121 RBI, Beltre became a free agent. He wanted to stay with the Dodgers, but they balked at the asking price of agent Scott Boras.

The Seattle Mariners did not and signed him to a five-year

contract worth nearly $65 million.

He was miserable.

The first time I interviewed Adrian was in the spring of
'05, and he was earnestly explaining how happy he was to be
a Mariner. When I asked him something about Los Angeles,
tears came to his eyes.

"I never wanted to leave," he said. "Baseball is a game and
a business, and the business part can break your heart."

Beltre devoted himself to the game in Seattle, making
friends quickly, becoming a popular teammate and go-to guy
for the media. Seattle's ball park, Safeco Field, worked
against right-handed hitters like Beltre, and in his five seasons there he never hit more than 26 home runs or had more
than 99 RBI.

Always, he was delightfully quirky. A free swinger, Beltre
would occasionally take a pitch against his better instinct –
and do a little dance of frustration in the batter's box, moving his feet up and down.

Fans found it charming.

He involved teammates – including young staff ace Felix
Hernandez – in a complicated contest called "flip" that began
with as many as 10 players in a circle, all wearing their
fielding gloves.

One player would throw the ball in the air and it would
suddenly be flying around the group, flipped from one player
at another.

When the ball hit the ground, someone was eliminated –
either the player who didn't catch it or the one who flipped it
but made it impossible to catch.

Beltre made the rules and was the final judge of all
disputes. What made his teammates laugh was his daily
changing of the rules, almost always managing to keep
himself in the game.

On the infield, Beltre would take a bucket of ground balls hit by coaches each afternoon, often working on his knees to maintain quickness of his hands.

And Beltre won Gold Gloves for fielding excellence – and then showed why he'd had to.

In August, 2009, White Sox shortstop Alexi Ramirez hit a hard ground ball to third base and the ball hit Beltre squarely where we all assumed his protective cup was.

He picked up the ball and threw to first base, and when the game went 14 innings, he continued playing.

Afterward, he went to the training room and was diagnosed with a "contused right testicle" – a phrase I'd never written in 30 years covering the game.

"I thought, 'it exploded,'" Beltre said of the impact of, well, ball-on-ball. "It was weird, because it hit right on it, right on top of it. I felt like going down, but I saw the ball right next to me, and I wanted to finish the play."

Why, I asked, wasn't he wearing his cup?

"I never wear one," he said – and I believe every male reporter in the room gasped. "I could never get comfortable."

Most astonishing? When Beltre came off the disabled list, the Mariners insisted he begin wearing a cup. For a game or two, he did, but then he went "commando" again.

"I can't play third base if I'm not comfortable moving or bending, and that's the first time I've ever really taken a direct hit," he said.

When his contract with Seattle ended, Beltre signed with Boston for one year, then with Texas for five years and $80 million.

By baseball's skewed standard, he may have been worth it.

Without a cup, his defense remains the best in the game. In his first two years away from Safeco Field, Beltre hit a combined 60 home runs and had 207 RBI.

In Texas, I asked Beltre if he still took buckets of ground balls every day at age 32. He made a motion toward his groin and grinned.

"Yes," he said. "And no, I still don't wear a cup."

Juan Beniquez: The Fearful Flyer

Juan Beniquez was a talented fourth outfielder for most of a career that spanned exactly 1,500 major league games. Few people aside from his teammates knew what he suffered for each of those games.

He played for seven teams, and each of them had road trips. Beniquez dreaded each trip.

All his life, he'd been afraid to fly. Not nervous, not reluctant – terrified.

Trainers gave him pills, Beniquez even tried drinking before take-off. Nothing helped, so he endured.

After climbing aboard every airplane he ever boarded, Beniquez would take a seat as far back in the cabin as was possible.

Anything bad, he reasoned, would likely start at the front of the plane.

He would begin to sweat when the doors to the aircraft closed.

As the plane taxied, Beniquez would seize the arms of his seat until he was nearly vibrating with the effort.

And for more than 17 seasons in the majors, he did the same thing every time he was aboard an airplane that started down the runway.

"Up, up, up!" Beniquez would scream.

Teammates laughed every time. A few minutes after take-off, Beniquez would often be asleep.

Landings never bothered him. He understood gravity, he said. Coming down was natural.

What he never fully accepted was that any airplane he was aboard would actually take flight.

Yuniesky Betancourt: Nice Guy Who Fell Short

The story Yuniesky Betancourt told us of his escape from Cuba in a boat that drifted off course for days before washing ashore in Mexico was, we sportswriters agreed, too good to be true. But we wrote it.

Betancourt had a child-like innocence, spoke through an interpreter and didn't really want to talk much about the huge waves and shark fins he saw and survived.

After all, by the time we met him, he was 23-years-old, had just signed a nearly $4 million contract with the Seattle Mariners – and all he wanted to talk about was playing big league baseball.

It was the reason he'd left Cuba and his family. It was the dream of his lifetime. And here he was.

The first time I talked to Yuni, I asked him what he liked most about his first spring training.

"Everything!" he said, and dropped a megawatt smile.

During his years in Seattle, my relationship with Betancourt was always friendly. No matter how frustrating his play – and his post-game comments – might be, he was a kid far from home who missed his mother and grandmother.

He never seemed happier to me than before games, when he'd sit on a couch with teammates watching a game or movie. Betancourt would literally snuggle himself into the group like a pup seeking warmth.

On the field, he was a colt, quick but unreliable. He would

make a play at shortstop that dazzled, then field a routine one-hopper and throw it into the stands.

At the plate, if the ball was thrown, Yuni was going to swing at it. He saw fewer pitches per at bat – just over three – than anyone in baseball. One year he walked 3 percent of the time.

Still, I would tease him, insisting he speak at least one word of English to me each day. Usually, after much jabbering, he would.

In 2007, agent Gus Domingez was charged with immigration violations – smuggling Cubans into the United States. And Betancourt was one of the men he'd brought in.

Betancourt had to testify against his former agent and tell the truth, which was no less harrowing than the story he first gave us.

At 22, he'd boarded a speedboat in Cuba and gone to Miami, where he was met by Dominguez representatives who then drove him across country to Los Angeles – then into Mexico.

All Betancourt wanted was to play baseball. In Mexico, he was arrested for carrying a false passport and jailed. Released back into the U.S., he signed a deal with the Seattle Mariners.

By 2005, he was in the majors.

Dominguez was convicted in 2007 and sentenced to five years in prison. Eventually, Betancourt was able to bring his mother and grandmother to Miami.

"I got them a nice house and we all live together," he said, beaming. "The smells of the food cooking in the kitchen, those are the smells I missed most."

What the Mariners believed would happen with experience never did for Yuni. He would swing at pitches in the dirt and pitches over his head.

Manager after manager, hitting coach after hitting coach worked with him to no avail. Even teammates grew frustrated with him – in key at-bats that might change a game, Betancourt was too impatient to make a pitcher work.

In 2009, Betancourt had gone from 175 pounds as a rookie to 215 pounds and his range at shortstop diminished. He tended to play the game unconsciously – unaware of the situation, oblivious to where teammates were.

On a June night that year, on a pop fly into shallow left field, Yuni ran all out and – despite being called off the play by outfielder Endy Chavez – made an over the shoulder catch.

As he made the catch, however, he and Chavez collided. Chavez's knee was all but destroyed, and he wouldn't play again for more than a year.

Yuni felt bad that Chavez was hurt, but couldn't understand why most felt it was his fault.

A few weeks later, manager Don Wakamatsu benched Betancourt for lackadaisical play. Yuni's response was, instead of taking more ground balls during practice, to take none. He just stood in the outfield with his arms crossed.

"I've done nothing wrong," he told me through an interpreter. "No one asked me to take ground balls. I have taken ground balls all my life, I don't need to show them I can catch a ground ball."

Not long afterward, Yuni was traded to Kansas City and, a year later, traded by Kansas City to Milwaukee.

Each time I encountered him after that first trade, Yuni would throw his arms wide, smile and embrace me. In spring training, I was to be on a sports talk radio show being done live from a bar, and Betancourt was there.

I got my hug. He even cheered when I want on-air.

For me, Yuni was impossible not to like. He wasn't a

particularly good big league ball player, and he certainly didn't have the work ethic of, say, teammate Adrian Beltre.

What I often wondered, though, was how many of those in major league baseball would have been willing to leave their friends, family and homeland – knowing they could never return – and hop in a small boat to cross 90 miles of ocean.

Yuni did that to play baseball.

Whatever scouts and teams saw in him was enough to make him millions of dollars. They assumed he'd grow, improve, adjust.

Yuniesky Betancourt never did. That didn't allow him to become the player he might have been, but it didn't make him a bad guy, either.

Willie Bloomquist: Pushed By Dad To Be His Best

All his life, Willie Bloomquist was a baseball player and his father, Dr. Bill, a dentist whose passion was coaching his children in whatever they took up.

"When one of the daughters began riding horses, she was quite good," a neighbor recalled. "I don't think Bill had ever been on a horse, but he was determined to tell her how to go about it."

With Willie and Bill, it was different. Dr. Bill was his son's coach in Little League, in travel ball. He knew and loved the game, loved the way his son played it – all out, always – and never stopped coaching him.

Signed by the Seattle Mariners out of Arizona State, where he'd been an All-American, Willie Bloomquist had always been the best player on every team he'd been part of.

In mid-summer, 2002, Bloomquist was struggling in Class AAA, a 24-year-old tasting failure for the first time on the field. Father and son clashed.

"He wanted to motivate me, but I wasn't in the mood," Willie said. "He said 'This game is too damned tough—you'd better go back to med school.' He kind of implied I'd gotten married and gotten soft.

"I said, 'I'm through talking to you.' The next day I started on a tear at the plate. My dad thought it was because he'd motivated me. I thought it was because I'd stopped listening to him."

For the first time in their lives, a barrier existed between father and son. That September, Willie was called up to make his major league debut, and in 12 games batted .455.

With his dad in the stands, Bloomquist went 4-for-4 in his first game.

When the season ended, Willie and wife Lisa took a cruise. Walking along the Cayman Island, Willie told his wife he had to make amends with his father, make it clear he loved him, appreciated his help.

At the same hour, Bill Bloomquist and a friend were going elk hunting, but swerved off the road in an accident that broke Bill's neck. Willie called his mother the next morning just to check in and heard the news.

He and Lisa flew to Utah to be with Bill. Bill talked and joked with them, but during a routine exam had a heart attack and went into a coma. A few days later, the hospital advised the Bloomquist family that if Bill didn't come out of it within 72 hours, he probably wasn't going to.

"It wasn't supposed to be like this," Willie told his mother, Dayna. "It's not supposed to be over yet."

Three days later, with no change, the Bloomquist family decided to gather in Bill's room the next morning and say goodbye. Then, 68½ hours into that 72-hour window, Bill Bloomquist woke up.

"The neurologist came in and said, 'This I've got to see,'" Willie said. "She'd written him off."

Initially, all Bill could do was blink his eyes in response to questions – once for yes, twice for no. Slowly, he seemed to regain himself, and his life became one rehab session after another.

Bill's memory never completely returned, and his short-term memory was worse.

"I showed him the video of my first big league hit on a

tape the team sent me," Willie said. "He got all excited for me. I showed him the next at-bat – another hit – and said, 'Now I'm 2-for-2.'

"He couldn't remember seeing the first hit 30 seconds before."

Bill Bloomquist's life, and those of his wife and children, changed forever in those first months.

"I told him what I wanted to say to him," Willie said. "I learned there are more important things than baseball. Last year, I had the best month of my life on the field – and a few weeks later, I didn't even care about it."

Bloomquist made the big league team the next spring, and every spring thereafter, as a jack-of-all-positions utility player. He was as adept in the outfield as at second base or shortstop and often played as many as seven positions a season.

Five years later, Mariners team president Chuck Armstrong talked about Bloomquist's abilities and drive.

"Willie has become the best utility man in baseball," he said.

And off the field, in a big league clubhouse?

"Willie is an old-fashioned red ass," general manager Bill Bavasi said. "And I mean that as a compliment."

Driven hard by his father throughout adolescence, Willie played with a chip on his shoulder. He hated losing, hated not playing as often as he wanted, loved any opportunity to make a difference in a game.

With his dad no longer able to serve as his coach, Bloomquist learned from teammates.

"Mark McLemore helped me learn how to prepare for pinch-running, playing different positions," Willie said. "John Mabry and Greg Colbrunn told me about the mental side of coming off the bench.

"Bret Boone taught me about obligations to your team,

about being the same guy the day after a loss that you were after a win. And Edgar Martinez taught me how to be a professional."

In the first 10 years of his career, Bloomquist played just under 900 games for five teams. After his heart attack, Bill Bloomquist attended less than a handful.

"I always knew my dad loved me, but it was hard sometimes, growing up," Willie said. "It wasn't just me, it was all four of us kids. He loved us, and he pushed us. It was part of his nature.

"If my father knew I was thinking more about him than about my job, he'd come unglued."

Mike Blowers: Lived The Game On Field And Off

Mike Blowers was a throwback to an era baseball had lost by the '90s – a time when players loved the game and the clubhouse and had trouble leaving either behind.

On the field, he was tough, competitive and smart enough to know both his strengths and his limitations. He knew what pitches he could hit, and talked to better hitters – like Edgar Martinez – until he understood how he might best get those pitches.

Almost as much as playing the game, Blowers enjoyed talking about it. Teammates were family, brothers who could sit in a quiet clubhouse hours after the game, sipping beers and talking baseball.

In a pinch on the road, he'd even do that with writers.

We were never friends – players and journalists rarely are – but we were friendly. Once, after Randy Johnson threatened to punch me in one of his look-at-me-now rages, I'd told Johnson to feel free to try.

Amused, Blowers called me over to his locker.

"I got your back," he said, and winked. We both laughed – no one ever took Johnson seriously off the mound.

Away from the game, Blowers was a family man, a major league player who golfed at the public course near where he'd grown up.

By 1999, Blowers had played more than 700 major league games, made money playing in Japan and come back from a horrendous knee injury. Over that winter, he knew his career might be over.

As he rehabbed at his home in the Northwest, I was in Florida spending a few days with Mariners manager Lou Piniella for a story. One day, talking about the team, Piniella said he was looking for a right-handed hitting first baseman to spell Paul Sorrento.

"I'd love to get Mike Blowers back for that role, but I'm told he wants too much money," Piniella said.

I said I'd talked to Blowers a few weeks before, and that I thought he'd love to play for Piniella and the Mariners again but that he had been told by his agent that then-general manager Woody Woodward had no interest.

We stared at each other a moment. I asked to use Piniella's telephone.

I called Blowers from Tampa. Money, he said, was no object. Piniella was the manager who had first given Blowers the chance to play regularly – and in 1995, he'd rewarded him with 23 home runs and 98 RBI. He wanted to play for Lou again.

After I hung up, I told Piniella, who then called Woodward in Seattle. A few days later, Blowers was signed.

I didn't ask for a commission.

It was an easy telephone call to make after years of bouncing questions off Blowers – on and off the record. He never helped me break a story, but he'd given me perspective plenty of times, and made me laugh often.

Years after his retirement, we worked together on radio, where he'd become a thoughtful analyst. His love for the game was undiminished, as was his sense of humor.

Blowers was a good player because he worked at it, a great companion because it came naturally.

Bert Blyleven: A Burning Desire

It took Bert Blyleven 22 years to put together Hall of Fame numbers – then 14 years for voters to grudgingly elect a man they seemed able to overlook once he'd stopped pitching.

"I'd like to thank the voters for finally getting it right," Blyleven said after being elected.

On the mound he was all business, with a fastball Don Drysdale advised him to throw inside and a curveball Brooks Robinson said "could buckle your knees."

By the numbers, he was a freak of nature: 242 complete games, six seasons in which he pitched 275 innings or more, 60 shutouts. 287 career wins, a pair of World Series championships ...

Blyleven's statistics were always good enough for the Hall of Fame, but there were many voters in the media who found reasons not to vote for him.

Born in the Netherlands, raised in Southern California by a father who was laborer, Blyleven came to baseball with a work ethic learned at home – and a sense of humor that kept everyone around him on high alert.

On the days he wasn't pitching, Blyleven was an arsonist, perfecting the act of setting an unsuspecting victim's shoe-laces ablaze. He used a matchbook, gum and a willingness to crawl any length to reach his prey.

In the Kingdome, for instance, Blyleven noticed that Mariners coach Phil Roof always sat near the entrance to the home clubhouse when in the dugout. So he crawled through that entrance and – with Roof focused on the game being played – managed to do what only Blyleven could do.

From the press box, there was a lot of laughter when Roof suddenly came hopping out of the Seattle dugout, one of his shoes in flames.

Blyleven was so adept at setting fires, even after those around him gave him few opportunities, that when he pitched for the Angels the team had a clubhouse fire extinguisher labeled "In case of Blyleven—Pull!"

Easily bored by most questions he got from the press, Blyleven would torment writers with his answers.

Asked the secret to his dominant curve, Blyleven insisted it was because of his long fingers – which he insisted had grown when he was a child, sticking them in dikes back home.

When he set a major league record for home runs allowed, the media expected humility. Bert laughed about it, instead.

"It's pretty bad when your family asks for passes to the game and wants to sit in the left-field bleachers," he said. "But they want baseballs just like everyone else."

The workhorse of the staff for each of the five teams he pitched for, the innings – 4,970 of them – would take their toll. Injuries cost him all or part of three seasons.

He was caught on television giving a fan the finger one night in Minnesota. Two decades later, back with the Twins as a color commentator, he was suspended for five games for dropping two f-bombs on the air.

Blyleven hadn't realized he was on a live broadcast.

When he was finally elected to the Hall in 2011, columnist Mark Whicker had the best line.

"It had better be fire proof," he wrote.

Barry Bonds: Don't Take Him Personally

Follow Barry Bonds for more than a few days and the three words most often used to describe him – by friends, teammates and coaches – were "That's just Barry." Occasionally, they were meant to be complimentary.

I was taking photographs of Bonds with Ken Griffey Jr. chatting behind the batting cage one spring morning when Bonds loudly took issue with my presence. Bonds angrily started toward me, but Griffey softly laid a hand on his shoulder, nodded toward me and told Barry, "Don't kill him. He's one of my writers." They went back to their conversation. What had I done to upset Bonds?

"That's just Barry," Junior said.

One afternoon 3½ hours before a regular season game, Bonds was lounging in his clubhouse recliner when a Giants representative ushered in a 14-year-old reporter who had scheduled an interview with Bonds for a school paper.

Politely, the boy approached Bonds.

"Mr. Bonds, do you have a minute?" he asked.

"Yes, I do," Bonds said. "But not for you."

Bonds walked away into the training room, the boy burst into tears and then-manager Dusty Baker saved the situation by asking the boy into his office for a one-on-one interview.

"That's just Barry," Baker said. "Don't take it personally."

If Bonds seemed to go out of his way to shock with rudeness, he could also surprise with kindness.

The first year Griffey Jr. came to big league camp in Arizona, he was an 18-year-old with almost nothing in common with anyone else in the clubhouse.

Bonds called him at the Mariners team hotel from Pirates camp in Florida, and the two talked about life and baseball several times a week for the rest of the spring. When asked, Bonds told writers he thought Junior would far exceed his own career.

Why would an established star take the time to befriend a nervous rookie half a continent away?

"That's just Barry," Griffey said.

* * *

If it had ended at that, with Bonds just being the biggest ass in baseball, he'd have been inducted into the Hall of Fame despite feuding with everyone from his father to his teammates and peers.

It didn't, and Bonds – for all his marvelous talents – may be considered right up there with Ty Cobb as one of the game's pariahs. The difference?

Ty Cobb is in the Hall of Fame.

Bonds isn't and likely won't be. In an era that will forever be suspect because of performance-enhancing drugs, Bonds led that charge.

He finished his career with more home runs than anyone in baseball history, and then was convicted in 2011 of obstruction of justice for not quite telling a grand jury the truth.

The irony is that Bonds might have been the most popular player of his generation had he put just a little effort into it.

A smile, a bit of graciousness, a love of the game ...

As it turned out, that just wasn't Barry.

Bob Boone: A Know-It-All Who Knew It All

Bob Boone irritated some of my brethren in the media because he often seemed to believe he knew more than anyone interviewing him.

He probably did, so it never bothered me.

Boone was the second of a three-generation big league family, and while he grew up learning about baseball from being with his father, Ray, he also went to Stanford – and gave some thought to being a doctor.

A catcher for each of his 2,264 major league games, Boone wasn't a man who was told what pitches to call from the bench. Managers often considered him a field manager in the game.

Boone certainly thought so.

His relationship with pitchers was remarkable, in that no matter how well – or badly – they were pitching, he made them think they were doing even better.

He knew not just what they threw, but why they wanted to throw it, and what buttons to push in any of them when a push was required.

"From spring training on, I need to know what pitch they can throw for a strike – where I want it – at any time," Boone said. "I might not call that pitch all game, until we need an out.

"You need to know, when the bases are loaded and there are two outs and there's a big hitter up, can you give me *that* pitch now? If you can, you can win a lot of games."

In most clubhouses, ask a player about a teammate or an opposing player, and there would be either clichéd answers or an I-don't-talk-about-other-players response.

Once Boone trusted me, which took a full season, I could ask him about anyone and the background he often led me in one direction or another.

Once I asked him if the best the game ever got for him was getting a pitcher a win, who wouldn't have had it if Boone weren't catching, and he surprised me by pausing before answering.

"That's my job," he said. "Hitting a ball on the screws, that's probably the best feeling – from the time you're old enough to swing a bat until you're so old they won't let you swing anymore."

Boone played the most physically demanding position in the game for 19 seasons, and when he retired he'd caught more games than any catcher in history.

Two of Boone's sons, Aaron and Bret, followed him into the big leagues, and when he retired as a player he became a manager, then a special assistant to a general manager.

By the last time I saw him, Boone seemed comfortable that he was respected for his mind, in and out of baseball. He'd earned that, and my thinking so was probably one of the reasons we always got along so well.

Bret Boone: Call Him 'The Boone'

When you are known as "The Boone," it can be difficult to see the humility in a persona created to be larger than life.

Bret Boone struck those who didn't know him as cocky – or worse.

"People think I'm a clown, and I don't blame them," he said, then pointed at me. "I say these goofy things, you guys write them down and people think I'm serious.

"No one who knows me takes me seriously."

Except on the field, where the third-generation major leaguer was a three-time All-Star, a four-time Gold Glove winner and had one of the best three-year runs in history by a second baseman.

Between 2001-2003, Boone hit 96 home runs and accounted for 365 RBI.

By the time he began that stretch, Boone was 32-years-old and had played 10 seasons with four teams. As he came into his best years on the field, Boone created his clubhouse personality, which teammate Mark McLemore dubbed 'The Boone.'

He would hold court before games, making sure to include himself in outrageous rants while often taking on the air of a man above the mere mortals he associated with.

Members of the media were 'clowns,' though it was hard to take offense when he made it clear he considered himself one, too.

I'd known him at age 12, when I was covering the Angels

and he and his brother Aaron were at spring training with their father, catcher Bob.

Another beat writer, John Strege, and I shared a condo which happened to be in the same complex as the Boones. One afternoon we watched Bret and Aaron playing wiffle ball in the quad.

Somehow, it became the media vs. the Boone boys.

One of my least-known talents is throwing a knuckleball with a plastic wiffle ball and making it dance. Young Bret then, as years later, had a tendency to swing ridiculously hard at times.

I struck him out with a knuckler. He was not pleased.

Next at-bat, I fed him another one – and he hit it over the roof of a second-floor condo. After that, we were friends.

Boone was a rookie in 1992, a soft-hands, big-swing infielder from USC, when we next ran into one another. I took him to lunch that spring, and he was appropriately humble.

"I look at guys like Ken Griffey Jr. and shake my head," he said that day. "To have that much talent, to be able to do what he's done so quickly ... it's amazing. It's not human.

"I just want to make the team."

Traded away in the winter of '93, Boone had a solid career before returning to Seattle in 2001. He'd grown up in a major league clubhouse – dad Bob and grandfather Ray knew and talked the game all his life.

Upon his return, I checked in with him.

"We don't all get it at the same time," Boone said. "Look at Jamie Moyer. Ten years ago, he was a No. 4 or No. 5 starter in someone's rotation. Now he's an ace, an All-Star.

"Jamie got it late in his career. I think it's clicking for me now. I changed my diet last winter, my training habits. I worked on my swing with my dad."

Once other players – and other writers – began arriving, I

watched Boone change that spring. One minute he was the kid I'd seen 20 years earlier, the next moment a different being entirely.

Manager Lou Piniella, wondering if Boone was versatile enough to play a little third base, put him there in a spring training lineup. Boone saw it and shook his head.

"The Boone don't play third base," he said.

Piniella changed the lineup.

And that's how it began. Always, tongue firmly in cheek, Boone became The Boone. Teammates egged him on – and it didn't take much.

One team flight, he turned a towel into a makeshift cape and ran down the aisles as 'Super-Boone.'

Another day, I happened to wander into a clubhouse dissertation on baseball talent, position-by-position. Virtually the entire team was gathered around Boone listening.

"The best athlete on the team is the shortstop," he said. "The second baseman is the next best athlete, he just doesn't quite have the arm to be a shortstop.

"First and third basemen? They're infielders who can't play up the middle – they're not that good – so you stick at the corners and hope for the best."

What about outfielders? Mike Cameron asked.

"Outfielders are the guys who don't have the talent to play infield, so you keep them as far away from the ball as you can," Boone said.

Ben Davis asked about catchers. Boone shook his head sadly.

"You play catcher when they've given up all hope that you can play anywhere else," he said. "And they're so afraid you'll hurt yourself, they give you a mask and chest protector and shin guards. They don't think you can stop the ball before it hits you."

Pitchers, someone said.

"All they have is an arm," Boone said. "They can't hit. They can't field. They have to stand on a hill to have any chance at all …"

Throughout that spiel, the Mariners roared with laughter. I ducked into manager Piniella's office. He was smiling.

"Boone?" he asked.

"No," I said. "The Boone."

Four years later, his abilities diminishing, Boone was released by Seattle and signed with the Minnesota Twins. He went there as Bret Boone – The Boone, he said, had been a product of the Mariners clubhouse.

What he found, in 14 games with the Twins, was that the love of the game and joy of the clubhouse weren't the same. He had been the star attraction in a three-ring circus with Seattle.

He'd been The Boone, and played the role so well – on and off the field – that being a member of the supporting cast wasn't enough.

Boone retired.

I have seen more talented players. What I have never seen is a three-year stretch where a team was so transformed by one goofy personality, who happened to be a player capable of carrying a team on the field.

"Nobody in our family is like Bret," brother Aaron said. "I'm not sure anyone on the planet is."

Chris Bosio: Speed Is Not the Answer

If youth is wasted on the young, 95 mph fastballs are often wasted upon those who can throw them.

Chris Bosio threw one early in his career, and like a lot of young pitchers, he had no idea what to do with it.

"My first big league game, I came in as a reliever and I was seriously pumped," Bosio told me. "I was throwing 95-96 mph. The first guy I faced was Pete O'Brien, and I threw him that fastball. Before I could turn around, it was bouncing on the warning track.

"I remember thinking, 'That pitch got them out two days ago in Double-A ...'"

By the time Bosio realized a 96 mph fastball wasn't enough to get major league hitters out, he no longer had one. Fortunately for him, what his right arm lost, his brain gained.

What he'd learned was how to pitch and, as importantly, where to pitch. Tutored by old-school coaches and peers, Bosio found a mound presence and developed a slider, a curve and a changeup – and threw each at different speeds.

In a pinch, Bosio would invent a pitch.

"Say it was a hot day and you needed a double play," he said. "You don't have to go to your mouth to throw a spitter, you throw a 'sweat ball.' You use what you've got to work with, and a sweat ball can sink, get you that ground ball."

Knee injuries all but crippled him, but Bosio was never

one for excuses. He neither made nor accepted them. One morning in the clubhouse I was interviewing pitcher Erik Hanson, who was explaining why he'd had a bad season a year earlier.

"I gave up more than 100 ground ball singles, more than anyone in baseball," Hanson said.

Bosio, sitting nearby, stood up and tapped Hanson on the shoulder.

"Get over it," he said.

Bosio's pitching philosophy was based on competition. A man who would put a fastball under anyone's chin, he was not beyond challenging hitters simply to do so.

He enjoyed the game, and gave it all his heart and legs would allow. His last season, Bosio could barely move off the mound. Not even 'sweat balls' could help him.

So he worked with Seattle's young pitchers that year, trying to pass on what he'd been taught more than a decade earlier. And before games, he softened a long-standing rule and began talking to opposing players.

Bosio asked me to take photographs of him with players he'd long battled and admired. At the end of that season, he offered to pay for all the film I'd shot that year. To him, that was what a professional player did – he paid for favors rather than demand them.

In a career that spanned 11 years, Bosio won 93 games and laughed a lot. He suffered nine major knee injuries, threw a no-hitter and occasionally brawled on the field.

When he retired, it wasn't by choice. He'd given everything he could, the tank was empty, and he knew it. I asked him if he'd have been a better pitcher if that 96 mph fastball had stayed longer.

"No," he said. "I was a better pitcher without it."

Jim Bouton: He Changed The Game's Image

Jim Bouton is the uncle everyone likes but no one wants to be cornered by at a family gathering. There is nothing he hasn't done, little he hasn't seen and no one he doesn't know.

If Bouton is more than willing to remind you of all that, there is one consolation – most of it is legitimate. The man was a major league pitcher, a best-selling author, co-starred in a popular Hollywood movie, and did the 11 o'clock news.

He also changed the way millions of people looked at baseball.

A good many baby-boomer sportswriters owe their perspective – and their careers – to "Ball Four" and the Bouton books that followed it. Irreverent and hilarious, they gave a nation of sports fans the first true look at what the inside of a big league clubhouse is like.

It's hard to imagine a book on baseball today creating the furor Bouton ignited. Newspaper coverage now can be more revealing than anything he wrote in 1970s. Bouton's players popped greenies and were profane, and a big league clubhouse was revealed as a place of real emotion and hilarity.

Bouton's players were human – and American's sporting public was shocked.

Bouton's baseball was a game of a more innocent time, but his clear love of it – along with the ability to laugh at himself – altered the way the media covers baseball.

For all he has done since leaving the game, Bouton

remains as fascinated by the clubhouse as any of the writers he inspired. A few years ago at Yankee Stadium, an almost shy Bouton waited outside the visiting clubhouse after asking to see Lou Piniella.

He wanted badly to go inside, to be part of all of it again, yet understood he could not. Most of the Mariners that day didn't know who Bouton was.

Bouton, the man can be gratingly self-serving, but as a lucid and insightful observer he changed the way a generation of writers viewed their craft.

That's a fair trade for a bit of pretentiousness.

Larry Bowa: Not So Nice, But Not So Bad Either

The first time I met Larry Bowa I was less than charmed. I'd walked into the Chicago Cubs spring clubhouse to interview reliever Lee Smith, and as we sat on stools and began talking, Bowa suddenly appeared at my shoulder.

"Don't talk to the fuckin' media," Bowa said. "They'll screw you every time. Fuck 'em.'"

Smith smiled, and when Bowa walked away simply shook his head and continued the interview. I thought a lot more of Smith than I did Bowa that day. Over the years, when Bowa coached and then managed, I had a few other encounters – none as glaring as the first – but wasn't surprised by his growing reputation.

So when Lou Piniella hired Bowa to coach third base in Seattle, I was prepared to dislike him for old times' sake.

Coach Bowa was totally unlike Bowa the player or Bowa the manager. He cared about his infielders – working one-on-one with them on his own as early as 7 a.m. on spring infields. He was tough but fair. And he didn't seem to mind the press.

Bowa had played in some tough media centers, Philadelphia and Chicago, and his in-your-face personality had been an easy target. His value to a team wasn't obvious. He was never a great offensive player, though he played 16 seasons and had 2,191 hits, but those he played with said he made good teams better.

"When Larry is on your team, no one ever relaxes," Smith told me.

Bowa told me our first encounter had been in keeping with his image in Chicago and I shouldn't have taken it personally. Once he'd been branded an obnoxious red ass, he kind of liked the fact that it got him out of the burden of talking to the press.

"They didn't like me, they didn't talk to me," Bowa said. "I thought that was a fair trade."

After he was hired to manage in Philadelphia, I walked into his office alone one afternoon to chat.

"Get the fuck out of here, I don't talk to the media until 5 p.m," he told me.

I started to turn away.

"Kidding," he said, and winked.

Milton Bradley: At War With His Demons

During early batting practice one afternoon on the road, someone set off a firecracker under the stands in left field, and most of the players on the field glanced in that direction.

Milton Bradley hit the ground.

"Where I grew up, you heard that sound, you instinctively went down," Bradley said. "I saw guys who didn't. They were the ones who got shot."

Bradley's baseball abilities were sizeable – a combination of speed, hand-eye coordination and strength – but throughout his 11-year career he never played more than 216 games with any one team.

And he played for eight.

Early on, Bradley's athleticism caught the attention of then-Mariners manager Lou Piniella, who saw a switch-hitter with immense potential. Seattle scouts knew all about Bradley.

"He's crazy," one said. "I don't mean goofy, I mean crazy."

There were incidents that seemed to make a case for it – emotional explosions that involved managers (Cleveland), umpires (San Diego), media (Texas) and fans (Seattle).

At each stop, plenty of people tried to befriend and defend Bradley, whose personality seemed bipolar.

When he joined the Mariners in 2010, he wanted nothing to do with the press.

I found Bradley fascinating and wouldn't leave him alone.

I made a point each day of saying "Hello, Milton." Inevitably, he would say "Hello" in return. Eventually we graduated to this: I would talk to him, off the record.

I wouldn't take notes, wouldn't quote him.

When Bradley was in the mood, the conversations had depth beyond sports. We talked about race, psychology, discussed people we'd each met and those we both wished we had.

Occasionally, Bradley would talk on the record, about a game or teammate, a situation or one play.

Milton Bradley was never dull. Nor was he ever far from a dark mood.

A first-time manager with Seattle, Don Wakamatsu reached out to Bradley, fiercely defended him in the media and broke camp with him as his starting left fielder in 2010.

Less than a week into the season, Bradley flipped the finger to a fan in Texas – and was caught doing so on television. A month later, Bradley asked the team for help dealing with anger issues and sought counseling.

The demons he fought were never far from the surface.

In the spring of 2011, I e-mailed Bradley, as I had done a dozen times before. The response stunned me.

"The media is going to drive me from the game," he wrote. In a 15-minute span, I got six e-mails from him. If he could only be left alone to play ball ... how was the new manager, Eric Wedge, selected and what had he said about Bradley?

Milton Bradley smiled when we first met that spring. I was glad to see him, wished him the best.

A few days later, he stopped saying "Hello." I had written nothing, done nothing, but we never spoke again. In May, the Mariners released him.

Bradley didn't say goodbye to anyone in Seattle.

Darren Bragg: Roses and Remembrance

For the longest time, Darren Bragg held the rose in his hand, feeling that to drop it at the grave would be to say goodbye forever.

He was 16 and a tough kid from Connecticut – the kind of baseball player even boarding school coaches called "scrappy." Raised by his mother after a divorce when he was young, Bragg found in baseball a passion he could share with the father he idolized.

"We didn't live together, but he never missed a game," Bragg said.

Little League. Pony League. High School. There were games of catch on the beach, long talks about the game. And then William Bragg missed his son's American Legion game – and before it ended, Darren Bragg knew something was wrong.

His father had died that afternoon. He would never see his son play collegiate baseball, make the USA team, get drafted, or start as a leadoff hitter for the Seattle Mariners on opening night, 1995.

At the funeral, the family held roses. Bragg couldn't drop his for the longest time. Two years later, he walked into a tattoo parlor, saw a small cross surrounded by three roses and had it put on his left arm.

It was Bragg's way of never saying goodbye.

"I play the game because I love to, but I play it for both of us," he said. "If I get a hit, I think of him. I like to think he's still watching me."

Built more like a bull dog than a whippet, Bragg made the majors at 5-foot-9, 175 pounds. He didn't excel in any single aspect of the game, but he could play the outfield well and had the speed to steal his first nine bases in Seattle without being caught.

Bragg played with perpetually bloodied knees, challenging walls and opposing pitchers. In Lou Piniella, he found a manager as tough as he was.

One night in Baltimore during that '95 season, Piniella kept Bragg in the clubhouse after the rest of the team departed to work on hitting. What Piniella wanted was to see Bragg go after the ball with more ferocity.

"Throw the bat at the ball, throw the bat head out there," Piniella screamed at one point.

And Bragg did – sending the bat pin wheeling through the clubhouse, shattering a wooden cubicle.

"That's more like it," Piniella said. "Now do the same thing at home plate, only hold on to the bat."

Bragg held on, playing with six major league teams in his first five seasons. Better players never got as far, but Bragg's toughness and passion for the game were as obvious as the tattoo on his left arm.

"I'll play until no one asks me to," Bragg said. "It's something I've loved most of my life, and something I've shared with my father every day I've put a uniform on."

Bill Buckner: An Error, Closure And Forgiveness

Bill Buckner played 22 years in the major leagues, 2,517 games, and for the casual fan is remembered for one play – an error – that followed him throughout his life.

It came in the World Series, which he'd helped the Boston Red Sox reach. In the ninth inning of game six, with Boston ahead and a win ending the series, a ground ball rolled through Buckner's legs and tied the World Series, 3-3.

In the seventh game, the New York Mets won, and Buckner's error was forever tied to their comeback.

He was a proud man, playing on devastated legs. A 1975 broken ankle needed several surgeries and ended up developing a staph infection. It made a gifted outfielder a first baseman-designated hitter at age 25.

"Everyone has things happen in their life they wish hadn't," Buckner said. "Mine happened on a baseball field, and they were nothing compared to what most people deal with in their lives."

For the remaining five years of his career, it was a rare day when Buckner's error wasn't brought up, from the stands or from the media.

For a time, he would say that being on the field in the ninth inning – a man with limited range and mobility – had not been his choice, hinting that he should have been replaced by a better defensive player.

It was true, but Buckner felt he was only throwing then-manager John McNamara under a bus, and he liked Mac. He dropped that defense. Buckner was tough enough to carry the weight alone.

How tough? Early in his career he collided in the outfield with teammate Bobby Valentine and fractured his jaw. Buckner had it surgically wired shut – and missed only one game.

One ankle had no cartilage because of that staph infection, the other was all but ruined and he played with a partially torn Achilles tendon. When he played with the Angels, teammate Brian Downing – an expert on playing in pain – was awed by Buckner.

"He works three, four hours a day to keep that ankle loose or it locks up," Downing said. "You watch him run hard, it's not pleasant. But what he goes through afterward is worse."

Buckner played with braces, tape and high-topped shoes to support his ankles.

And through all the years he played that way, he had 2,715 hits, 498 doubles, 49 triples, 174 home runs, 183 stolen bases.

How?

"From the time I was 5 or 6 years old, this is what I planned on doing with my life," Buckner told me late in his career. "What you go through to play – the surgeries, the pain, the hours on ice – is part of the cost.

"People don't understand that, but then they don't get the joy of playing, either.

"Most of my life, 3,000 hits was my goal. If I'd been healthy, no problem. As it is, I'm trying to squeeze as much out of my body as I can before it ends."

When it ended, Buckner retired to Idaho, where the media didn't write about the '86 World Series. After a few years, he missed the game and returned as a batting coach in Chicago.

"I played in parts of four decades, and that was important to me," he said with pride. "I paid a price for that, physically, but it was worth it to me. I loved this game."

In 2008, Buckner was invited back to Boston to throw out the ceremonial first pitch and accepted.

"The media in Boston was hard on me, but the fans were always supportive," he explained. "If I get booed, I get booed."

When Buckner was introduced and walked slowly to the mound on a surgically fused ankle, Red Sox fans stood and gave him a two-minute ovation that brought tears to his eyes.

Asked afterward what that ovation felt like, Buckner shook his head.

"Closure," he said. "Forgiveness."

Jay Buhner: The Buzzcut King

By the late '90s, only 10 men in major league history had hit 40 or more home runs in three consecutive seasons. Fewer still had run happily through the clubhouse wearing nothing but a bagel on his private parts.

Jay Buhner did both.

In a career fraught with injuries, he played 15 years but only four times played as many as 150 games, and retired with 310 home runs.

The men who played with him counted on two things from Buhner: That he would play every game all out, and that off the field they had to be very careful around him.

Why?

A young Japanese right-hander, Makoto Suzuki, was in his first spring with Seattle and was sitting on a training room table when Buhner walked in, vomited on that table, and left.

"Makoto wouldn't come into the training room after that," team trainer Rick Griffin said.

"There is no one in Japan like Buhner," Suzuki told me.

I believed him.

Buhner was a marvelous right fielder who may have crashed into as many fences as he hit balls over. He paid a terrible price, physically, for his style of play and his personality.

In May of 1994, for instance, he nearly blinded himself.

"I'd gone 0-for-something and I was mad. I had tape on my left wrist and I was trying to get it off with a tape cutter," Buhner said. "I yanked it right through and the momentum carried right on up to my forehead.

"The tape cutter stuck in my head just above my eye. The trainers were pretty upset."

Over the course of his career, Buhner fractured his forearm (twice), bruised his pelvis, blew out his left knee (surgery) and had a ligament taken from his left forearm to repair the one torn in his right elbow.

"I tore an Achilles tendon, sprained my ankle so badly I had bone chips afterward, broke the ulna bone twice, had surgery on my clavicle ..." he said, and then laughed.

"When I leave the game I'll have to detox – that's how many medications they have me on to keep me out there. Anti-inflammatory, muscle-relaxants, cortisone ..."

He lost his hair, so he shaved his head, a look that became so popular in Seattle that the Mariners hosted 'Buhner Buzzcut Night' with anyone showing up without hair – or who would allow on-site barbers to buzz them – getting in free.

"That was awesome," said Buhner, who would buzz at least one or two fans on those nights.

On the field, Buhner played until his body or the team doctor wouldn't allow it.

"There were times I shouldn't have played, did and had big games," Buhner told me. "Once, early in my career, we played a double-header in Detroit, and I hurt my knee in the first game and had to hobble around.

"I played the second game, had five RBI and we won. It taught me a lesson - you don't have to be at 100 percent to help your team."

Oh, but off the field.

Manager Lou Piniella had a notoriously weak stomach, and Buhner abused him for most of a full season. How? He'd sidle up to Piniella behind the batting cage during batting practice, start to talk to him and then – on cue – throw up.

Piniella would stagger off, holding his mouth.

"I couldn't hide from him, though I tried that for awhile," Piniella said. "I finally had to steel myself and not react. Once it didn't bother me, Jay found other ways to torture me."

Fiercely loyal to teammates, Buhner was also dead honest with me – even when he wouldn't let me quote him.

Staff ace Randy Johnson had gone from a good-humored clubhouse companion to a self-absorbed pitcher no one much cared for except every fifth day, when he pitched.

I compiled a list of things Johnson had done, from blaming his teammates for not scoring runs – and potentially costing him a Cy Young Award – to all but throwing games when he wanted to be traded from Seattle.

When the story ran, news stations descended upon the ball park to interview players. I handed Buhner a copy of my story before he went live on-air, and he read it and grinned.

"I got no problem with it," he said, "but now I got to go rip you on TV."

Beneath the bullish image, Buhner was a sensitive man, absolutely devoted to high school sweetheart-turned-wife Leah and their three children, Brielle, Chase and Gunnar.

Late in Buhner's career, Gunnar started having emotional issues with his father leaving so often, and Buhner and I would talk about the problems that jobs we loved caused our loved ones.

It weighed on him.

Seven years after Buhner retired, I had a heart attack, died on the table and was brought back by surgeons. With my wife and daughter visiting me, Buhner called the hospital room.

I couldn't talk yet. Jay talked to my daughter, Jessica.

"Your dad's a fighter, he's tough and he's going to make it back," he told her. "He's a good man and I love him."

Months later, back on the job, I ran into Buhner, who'd stopped by the ball park. We did the man-hug thing and I tried to tell him how much that call had meant to my family.

I teared up a bit. Jay did, too.

All the home runs and big catches took a backseat for me, and I realized with Buhner, they always had. What I'll always remember was the sweetness of that call to my daughter.

Well, that and seeing him prance around the clubhouse with a bagel around his ...

Ken Caminiti: Didn't Mind Getting Dirty

Walk into the spring clubhouse of the San Diego Padres at 7 a.m. or 6 p.m., and Ken Caminiti always seemed to be there. If he wasn't on the field, he was taping bats, joking with teammates, talking quietly with a reporter.

I never knew Caminiti away from the ballpark and club-house, but in that element he was gregarious and friendly – a man who kept his demons close and hid them well.

Teammates loved Cami, and with good reason. He played the way major leaguers played before it was marketable to be cool. Caminiti smiled on the field, scowled at himself after errors and strikeouts, and flung himself after any baseball that hit in his vicinity. If he wasn't dirty, he wasn't happy.

And he was almost always happy on the field.

Teammates remember him taking medication and water through an IV before one game because he'd become dehydrated, then playing and hitting a pair of home runs. Writers respected his willingness to talk after good games and bad.

No one knew how deep his problems were. Friends met his wife and three daughters and saw how he doted on them. If he occasionally showed up a little raw after a long night, it was nothing anyone in baseball was unfamiliar with – drinking was considered part of the game for decades.

What no one knew in time was that it wasn't just drinking. It was drugs, both performance enhancing and mind-altering chemicals, and Caminiti pursued them with the same fervor that he went after ground balls.

His last spring with the Padres, I walked over from the adjoining Mariners complex to give him a picture I'd taken of him. It was a little before 8 a.m., and the clubhouse was just beginning to fill up. Cami was at his cubicle, retying the strings on a new glove. He waved in recognition, and then took the photograph I offered.

"Man, that's a great shot, a great shot," he gushed. I told him I had 10 or 12 of him that were terrible, and he laughed. Caminiti was more than cordial, he had a genuine warmth that drew in everyone around him.

What we never suspected was how good he was at keeping everyone around him out. After that spring, Caminiti played with a few other teams and I saw him only a few more times.

Always, he'd wave and wink at me in the dugout or around the cage.

Late in October, 2004, I read about his court appearance in Houston, where he admitted violating his probation by using cocaine. This, after admitting he'd taken steroids as a player, and during his 1996 season for which he was voted the National League's Most Valuable Player.

"I had a real good thing going for me and I got sidetracked," he said that day. "It doesn't have to be drugs. It doesn't have to be alcohol. That part of my life is over."

Caminiti made you want to believe him, in the way that passionate addicts hide the truth from everyone they can. But his core was so solid – so decent – that you wanted to believe he could get past this and enjoy life after baseball.

Less than 10 days later, Caminiti was dead at 41.

Cause of death, according to the autopsy: "acute intoxication due to the combined effects of cocaine and opiates.

Rod Carew: Not One to Suffer in Silence

One of the great misconceptions about major league base-ball players is that some are too soft to play in pain.

Some are tougher than others but virtually everyone is hurt during a 162-game season. It may be a debilitating injury or a lingering ache, a bruise that won't heal or a sliding burn that won't close. Players all hurt. They all play hurt. Some suffer pain better than others.

Rod Carew was a sensitive soul who could lay wood on any pitch, a slashing line drive hitter and one of the better bunters in the game, a man who stole home more than any player of his generation.

His career would put him in the Hall of Fame, but Carew occasionally needed creative handling.

If he was sore, he would tell writers he had a torn muscle – and expect team trainers to back him up on the claim. Carew would play with pain, but he wanted everyone to know it and was at his happiest if the injury was exotic.

Once Carew awakened on the road with a stiff neck, a malady anyone who's ever slept in a hotel bed can relate to. He came to the ballpark early for treatment, the usual heat and massage.

By mid-afternoon, about the time the media began arriving, Carew was openly wondering if he would be able to play that night. Two trainers came up with what looked like a dog muzzle, snapped it in place over Carew's chin and jaw.

They attached elastic bands to it and took Carew into one of the stalls in the players' bathroom. There, seated on the toilet, one of the best contact hitters in history would tie the contraption to the bars of the stall and, by leaning forward, support his head and neck.

Players shook their heads at the sight. Even the trainers giggled. Manager Gene Mauch wrote Carew's name in the starting lineup. He knew.

Sure enough, Carew emerged slowly from the toilet stall and – once the press was on hand – was helped out of the muzzle.

"I've been in traction all afternoon," he told the media. "But I'm playing."

If eccentricity was part of his personality, Carew considered himself something of an artist among thugs. He cradled a bat with soft hands at the plate, ran almost daintily.

Carew's skills were impossible to duplicate. A dominating pitcher might shut down an entire lineup but allow three hits to Carew. He hit fastballs up the middle, sent sliders to the opposite field, pulled changeups and would drop a bunt for a hit in any count.

Many hitters were streaky, unable to make an out when things were going well, unable to make contact when they weren't. Carew rarely endured slumps of any length.

For most of his career, Carew felt misunderstood and under-appreciated, and probably was. He was kind and gracious with players he liked, distant with those he didn't. He could be thoughtful or tactless in the same interview. He loved his wife and family and other women, and saw that as his business.

What he wanted most was respect, and it hurt him deeply when he felt he didn't get enough of it. Carew played superbly with that pain most of his career.

Norm Charlton: Old School Tough

Norm Charlton graduated from Rice with a triple major – political science, religion and physical education – which meant talking to him in a clubhouse or over a beer hours after a game was always interesting.

He was old-school tough and didn't believe players should take their family to Disneyland or go golfing the day of a game.

"We get paid a lot of money to play baseball. Guys say they need to have a life, but we're not paid to have a life during the season," he told me. "I have a life in the off-season."

An avid hunter and fisherman, his love of animals produced odd bedfellows – sometimes literally.

In 1993, Charlton and his wife, Nancy, bought a 4,000-acre ranch an hour south of San Antonio and dubbed it the Charlton Cattle Co. They raised cattle and trophy deer – and had plenty of each.

They also adopted raccoons and a javelina that Nancy found when it was about the size of a tennis shoe.

"She bottle fed her and the first night the thing slept on the bed between us," Charlton said.

The orphaned creature of the Charlton Cattle Co. had run of the house for months before the javelina was ejected. From then on, she'd show up in the backyard and sleep in a chaise lounge.

In 1993, Charlton was also traded to Seattle from Cincinnati, and reunited with manager Lou Piniella, who'd managed the Reds to the World Series championship in '90.

Their personalities were similar. All that mattered in the end, was winning.

Charlton appeared in 34 games his first year with the Mariners, saved 18 of them, and destroyed his left elbow, requiring major reconstructive surgery.

He missed a year, signed with Philadelphia and pitched poorly enough to get released. Charlton made one phone call. He called Piniella.

"I knew he'd stick his neck out for me," Charlton said. "I knew he'd give me the chance to prove I could still pitch."

The Mariners signed Charlton on July 14, when they were a distant second in their division to the Angels. For the rest of the season, the Mariners closed the gap, and Charlton closed their victories.

In 30 games that season, he saved 14, won two others and the Mariners then won a one-game playoff with the Angels to win the American League West.

Charlton was nicknamed The Sheriff, and Seattle fans loved him. A year later, he saved 20 games but blew five saves, lost seven times and was one of the reasons the Mariners failed to make the post-season.

There were extenuating circumstances no one knew about until I visited the Charlton Cattle Co. that winter.

"In July, I called home from the airport one night and Nancy told me she was pregnant," Charlton said. "I was crying – guys were asking me if I was OK."

After 11 years of trying, the Charltons were pregnant.

Weeks later, from the road in Detroit, he called home but couldn't reach his wife. He called his sister-in-law who gave him the news – Nancy was in the hospital. She'd miscarried.

"I was crushed," he told me. "Then later that night, I went

to work."

Charlton didn't tell his teammates or Piniella, and that night he blew a save. Four nights later, he blew another one, then a third in a week.

What Charlton was going through was guilt.

It was a heart-breaking story that got worse.

The '97 season was a disaster for Charlton, who appeared in 71 games and finished with a 3-8 record, 14 saves and a 7.27 earned run average.

I knew something was wrong, if not physically then emotionally. For months, Norm wouldn't answer no matter how I asked. When he did, I almost wished he hadn't.

The fairy tale marriage had become a tragedy. The Charltons had divorced and gone their own ways.

Charlton pitched another four years, for Baltimore, Atlanta, Tampa Bay, Cincinnati, and then one last season with Seattle. We talked often, and slowly his life improved.

When he retired, it was to the Texas coast where he bought a couple of boats and became a fishing guide. Whenever he'd send a photo, he'd be on a boat in the sun, with a fishing pole, a big dog and a beer bottle next to him.

That always made me smile.

Jeff Cirillo: Too Sensitive For Tough Love

Jeff Cirillo was a sensitive soul *before* he met Lou Piniella, so the tough style of the Seattle Mariners veteran manager was never going to create a happy relationship.

Cirillo was a third baseman who, with the Colorado Rockies in 2001, had batted .313 with 17 home runs and 83 RBI. He was a career .300 hitter and had driven in 115 runs in 2000.

So when the Mariners sent three promising young pitchers to the Rockies for Cirillo, there was no reason to believe his bat wouldn't be productive in Seattle.

I knew better. The best general manager I ever covered, Pat Gillick, made the deal – but whatever scouting the team had done on Cirillo in Colorado apparently didn't include his personality.

"Jeff's a good hitter, but he's high-maintenance," a Rockies beat writer told me when I called.

Uh-oh. Piniella was an old school manager, had been an old school player, a guy who willed himself to success against those with more ability. He didn't do high maintenance.

Cirillo had talent – a natural swing and soft hands. He wanted the game to be stress free.

It was a recipe for disaster.

A week into their first spring camp together, Piniella didn't like anything about Cirillo's swing.

"You listen to the ball off his bat, it's like he's swinging a wet newspaper," Piniella said, making a sour face.

It got worse. By the time the regular season began, Cirillo would walk to the on-deck circle and Piniella would turn to one of his coaches and say – loud enough for Cirillo to hear.

"He's entered the circle of death."

In Piniella's world, a player confronted with that sentiment marched into his manager's office, slammed the door closed behind him and didn't come out until the two had reached an agreement. Piniella waited months for that confrontation.

It never came.

Cirillo wanted positive feedback, not needling. He'd felt appreciated in Colorado. He thought Piniella was a bully.

I liked Jeff Cirillo. I'd met all kinds of players in my career, all different. Cirillo wasn't the type to challenge Piniella, but we got along well and he was candid beyond the point most players were comfortable.

Early on in a road trip, we were chatting on the bench before batting practice and Cirillo said he was a little concerned because he'd forgotten to bring his antidepressants when the team left Seattle.

I wasn't sure he was serious – no player in the more than 20 years I'd then been covering baseball had ever mentioned taking an anti-depressant. I asked what he was taking.

Cirillo told me, and it was another surprise – it was the same medication I'd been taking for a year. We discussed dosages, and I offered to loan him a few pills. He had his shipped to him overnight.

But they would never be enough for him in Seattle. Piniella got in his head like a disapproving parent, and Cirillo spiraled on the field. His first year in Seattle, he batted a career-low .249.

"He hates me," Cirillo said of his manager.

A year later, Cirillo was hurt much of the season, and batted .205.

"He's killing me," Cirillo said. "I've got to get out of here."

There was a problem getting Cirillo out of Seattle, though no one thought his staying was a good idea. His 2004 salary was $6.9 million. GM Bill Bavasi, who'd inherited that contract, traded Cirillo and a lot of cash to San Diego for not much in return.

The ultimate irony for Cirillo was that the winter he was traded, Piniella left Seattle, too.

Cirillo played another five seasons, retired with a career .296 batting average. His career after Lou never approximated his career pre-Lou, but every time we ran into one another after he'd left Seattle, he was smiling.

Ken Cloude: Playing With Guilt

A few days removed from Class AA, Ken Cloude no-hit the Chicago White Sox for six innings and then beat the Baltimore Orioles – his hometown team – five days later for his first major league win.

A perfectionist, Cloude took an attitude to the mound that manager Lou Pinella loved, even when he hated it.

"I went to the mound one time, and I was hot. He was in a jam and I told him 'I don't like the way you're pitching,'" Piniella said. "And the kid yells right back at me, 'I don't like it any more than you do. Go sit down!'"

Piniella laughed at the story.

"He's tough, he has an attitude and he won't give in to anyone," Piniella said.

Cloude was 22 when he broke in with the Seattle Mariners, and never alone. His constant companion was his brother, Doug – and his guilt over Doug's suicide.

"We had baseball cards made of ourselves when we were kids, and I still carry his," Cloude said. "His initials are inside every cap I wear. And when I'm on the mound, I find myself looking into the stands at some point every game, thinking I'm going to see him."

They'd shared bunk beds throughout childhood, snuck off for early-morning fishing trips, talked to one another late into the night.

Baseball took Cloude away from Baltimore and his family.

"My first year in pro ball, we never got the chance to sit down and have a conversation," he said. "We should have. I was the lucky one, the older brother who was the best at a lot of things. That wasn't easy to follow for Doug."

Without leaving a note or any explanation, Doug Cloude hung himself in 1995. He was 19, Ken was 20.

Baseball never felt quite the same afterward.

"I love this game and I always will, but that's what it is, a game," Cloude said. "You go to great cities, play in great ballparks and get paid. But there are more important things in your life – or there should be.

"If I'd called Doug more often, if I'd known whatever it was he was going through, maybe it would have worked out differently."

Cloude made 71 major league appearances over his first 10 years in professional baseball, and his career was shadowed by horrific injuries. In 2000, he ruptured a ligament in his right elbow and underwent "Tommy John" surgery.

Seven months later, in agility drills, he tore an Achilles tendon and missed the entire 2001 season. The next season, he went 9-4 in Class AAA with 2.33 earned run average – then was sidelined by shoulder stiffness days before the Mariners were going to bring him back to the majors.

When Cloude left the organization following the 2003 season, only one team pursued him. He was 30 when the Tampa Bay Devil Rays signed him to a contract, and he hadn't thrown a pitch in the majors in four years.

Still, Piniella, now manager of Tampa, wanted Cloude.

"What he's gone through is amazing, and I don't think anyone knows what he could do if he could just stay healthy," Piniella said.

"Yeah, I wanted to give him a chance to do that, get healthy and pitch. But I'm not Saint Lou. Ken Cloude is still a tough guy on the mound.

"We're both a bit older now. Maybe we'll actually get along on the mound."

Cloude never pitched another major league game.

Ben Davis: Looking Good Was Not Enough

One night at the baseball winter meetings of 2001, with most of the general managers sleeping in their hotel rooms, Seattle Mariners manager Lou Piniella sat at a bar with San Diego GM Kevin Towers.

On the back of a napkin, the two men came up with a six-player trade that would make Ben Davis a Mariner.

There was never a man who looked any better in uniform than Davis, a 6-foot-4 well-defined 195 pounds. Jet black hair and just enough of a five o'clock shadow to look gritty.

The Mariners had a catcher, the durable Dan Wilson, but Wilson was aging and the team at some point would need a successor. To Piniella's eye, it might be Davis.

The second player taken in the 1995 amateur draft, Davis received a considerable bonus and commenced spending it on himself. He liked trucks and women, and women loved Davis.

What he didn't do in San Diego was hit. In a career-high 526 at-bats in 2001, Davis batted .239. The Padres had seen enough.

Davis was a teammate almost impossible to dislike – his love of fun in a clubhouse included a good-natured ability to take what anyone wanted to dish out.

"Big Ben Davis," Piniella would call as he walked through the clubhouse.

Every day, as the team went to stretch, Davis would build

a 'little man' on the Mariners bench out of his catching equipment. He'd prop up the shin guards below the chest protector, lean the protector against the back of the bench and then put his mask at top the chest protector.

The result: A mini-catcher.

It was about as much heavy lifting as Davis liked to do.

Before a game in his first spring with Seattle, Davis sat on the bench watching the team take infield – with two young catchers taking and making throws at the plate.

Wilson had the day off, Davis was starting, but he didn't want to participate in the pre-game workout.

Piniella walked into the dugout with a few of us beat writers in tow, answering questions about the team. I had known Lou for 10 years at that point, and could tell from his glances at Davis that he wasn't happy.

Finally, he couldn't stand it and asked Davis why he wasn't on the field with the rest of the team.

"I'm starting, so I wanted to give the young guys the work," Davis said.

Lou simmered another moment, and then turned back to his catcher.

"Well, as long as you're not doing anything, why don't you walk across the street to McDonald's and get us a couple of milk shakes," he snapped.

Davis didn't get it. He laughed. But it was the last time he skipped infield. It was only a minor improvement of the Davis work ethic.

By the end of Davis' first year in Seattle, Piniella would be talking to one writer or another in his office and – without prompting – suddenly make a sour face and say 'Big Ben-fucking-Davis.'

By age 27, Davis was out of the game and close to being out of money. At 31, he decided he'd come back – as a pitcher. Oddly, for a man who'd caught 486 games, Davis knew almost nothing about pitching. But he threw hard.

Davis signed a minor league deal with the Cincinnati Reds and seemed to grasp how much time and money he'd squandered. Now he had a wife and three children.

Pitching in a Class A game, he felt a pop in his shoulder and never threw well again.

He reminded me of the story of the grasshopper and the ant. The ant worked all summer while the grasshopper played the fiddle, singing "oh, the world owes me a living ..."

In the end, of course, the ant had food in the winter and let the starving grasshopper in and the grasshopper changed his tune.

I'm not sure Davis ever did. But my God, the man looked good in a uniform.

Tim Davis: Putting Big Payday In Perspective

Tim Davis was a 5-foot-11 left-handed pitcher who was a substitute teacher in the off-season of his first year with the Seattle Mariners – when he was paid the then-minimum big league salary of $120,000.

He was smart enough to realize his career might not last forever, given injuries that hampered him. One day as we walked from the team hotel to the Ballpark in Arlington, we talked about money.

Davis brought it up.

"It's a good salary, but people forget you have to establish two homes, one where you live, the other where you play, and maintain both all season," Davis said.

"And we get taxed not only in the state where we live, but now in every state where the team plays. They pro-rate what we make in the games we play here in Texas, then tax us on that income."

I listened, realizing all this was just occurring to Davis. He wasn't complaining, he was describing the wonder of it – making good money for the first time in his life, and watching it get nibbled away by factors he'd never taken into consideration.

At some point in our walk, he turned and asked me a question.

"Do you make the big league minimum?"

"Not hardly," I said. "If you combined all three beat

writers who travel, we'd make the minimum."

"Doesn't the team have to pay you the minimum?" he asked.

I explained I worked for a newspaper, not the Mariners.

"So you do all this for – what – less than $50,000 a year?" he asked.

"I do."

"You're crazy."

"Probably," I said, and we both laughed.

Tim never mentioned money to me again. His career lasted parts of four seasons. In his last year, at age 27, he was paid $227,000.

By 2011, the major league minimum salary was $414,500.

All these years, and I still don't make that.

Brian Downing: Didn't Make High School Team

The better I got to know Brian Downing, the more impossible his career seemed, and I got to know him well.

Not only didn't Downing play high school baseball, when he finally did try out at Cypress Community College, he couldn't crack the starting lineup.

Into his late teens, Downing would turn his backyard into a ballpark, using a hose for the base paths and hitting not balls but bottle caps, all while doing his own play-by-play.

His parents wouldn't sign the consent form allowing him to take drivers' education. His father, an aerospace worker who lost his job, spent Downing's teen years watching television in a darkened living room, growing his hair so long he kept it in a ponytail.

"You'll never make it," he told his son.

Downing so impressed his college coach – with hustle and a desire to learn – that he called an old friend, and Downing was signed by the Chicago White Sox and dispatched to rookie ball.

"I'd bag the balls after practice, carry equipment – anything, just to stay with a team," Downing told me.

He was 5-foot-10, about 150 pounds. Deep down, he feared his father was right.

Downing would play anywhere: catcher, third base, the outfield. I teased him once, saying he reminded me of a dog on the beach chasing a Frisbee – he didn't care who or what he ran over or through, he was going to try to make the catch.

"That's about right," he said. "My first game, I was sent in at third base, and there was a little pop fly near the dugout. I dove for the ball, went down the stairs and tore up my knee.

"They had to carry me off the field, but as I'm lying there, I hear the PA guy say, 'Now playing third base, Brian Downing.'"

In that first season, Downing was 23 and had never been on a date. A Chicago usher named Cheryl flirted with him, they went out.

Downing married her.

I've never known a man who changed more often while keeping his core the same. Downing realized, eight years into his professional career that he wasn't worth any more than the $50,000 a year he was paid.

He read up on weight training, worked out and gained 20 pounds of muscle. When he came to spring training in 1979, teammate Nolan Ryan spotted him in the clubhouse.

"I thought he was wearing a chest protector under his shirt," Ryan said.

The strength gave Downing a confidence he'd never had, and he batted .326 that season, hit 12 home runs. On the field, his career changed.

A kid who couldn't make his high school team, who didn't start in college, went on to hit 275 career home runs, drive in 1,073 RBI with an impossible 2,099 hits.

None of it satisfied him.

A broken ankle ended his catching career, so he went to the outfield where he literally could run wild. Downing careened into walls, fences and - once - a tarp roller, hitting it so hard in Milwaukee he thought he'd broken his thigh.

And that produced another oddity in Downing. He believed he played better when he was hurt. He would focus his rage, his pain on the opposing team.

I moved to Seattle, and Downing and the Angels came through the Kingdome one year. Downing was hurt, he'd strained his rib cage with one ferocious swing or another.

We went to lunch, caught up, laughed. I asked him how he could swing a bat and he smiled.

"I'm probably good for one, maybe two swings tonight," he said. "So I'll try to make them count."

That night, Downing was almost taken out of the game when he swung and missed in the first inning, the pain in his side obvious to everyone at the park.

He got through inning after inning and we arrived in the ninth inning tied. The Angels rallied, put a man on base and the game came to Downing. I watched him on deck, swinging tentatively, and I realized he thought he had that one swing left in him. I knew he was hurting.

I'd lifted weights with Brian, played two-on-two basketball with him, spent time at his home with his wife and children, driven from Phoenix to Palm Springs with him one spring.

And I knew his background, how much he carried a father's disapproval with him.

Downing went to the plate and with that one good swing homered to put the Angels ahead. In the press box, I had a lump in my throat. The ethics of the profession were that we never root for a team.

I never have.

What Downing taught me was that I could root for individuals, no matter what team they were with.

Over the years, I watched him try to learn to play blues guitar, take up the harmonica and, in another phase, dress in leathers and ride a Harley Davidson across country.

In the end, his career lasted 20 years. Impossible.

Dennis Eckersley: Passion and Precision

The night Dennis Eckersley threw a no-hitter in 1977, he didn't walk humbly into history. With one out in the ninth inning and two strikes on a hitter, Eckersley pointed to Jerry Remy in the on-deck circle.

"You're next," Eckersley screamed.

A year later he won 20 games and at 24 was on top of the world. He partied as hard as he threw, and it nearly ended his career. There were arm problems. Drinking problems.

By the time he turned 32, Eckersley had won 151 big league games but was considered done by the Chicago Cubs. They weren't off by much.

One night after Christmas, 1986, Eckersley and his then 10-year-old daughter were staying with in-laws, and Eckersley got drunk. It wasn't the first time. What he didn't know until the next morning was that his sister-in-law videotaped his evening.

"I saw the video the next morning and begged them to turn it off," Eckersley said. "They wouldn't turn it off, so I watched this drunk – me – make an ass of himself in front of his daughter."

Eckersley checked into rehab within a week.

Traded that spring, Eckersley was a setup man in the Oakland bullpen until closer Jay Howell needed surgery at the All Star break. Without many options, manager Tony LaRussa and pitching coach Dave Duncan gave Eckersley the ninth inning.

He never gave it back.

It wasn't that he was perfect in the role. Kirk Gibson and the Los Angeles Dodgers proved him mortal in the 1988 World Series. Eckersley could be beaten, but never for long.

He swore he pitched scared in every save situation ever handed him, that part of him stood on the mound each time and feared failure.

There was another part of Eckersley. One he admitted would watch himself from the stands and applaud as he put on a super hero's cape. Eckersley beat alcohol and the demons that pursued him throughout most of his young life.

On the mound, he was a combination of passion and precision. In 1989, he walked three batters in 58 innings. A year later, in 73 innings, he walked four batters.

Of all the players Don Zimmer coached or managed in his long career, Eckersley remained one of his favorites. His reasons were simple.

"Dennis played the game the way it was meant to be played, and it mattered to him," Zimmer said. "He had fun. He was competitive. And he loved being out there."

Cecil Fielder: It's Hard For Big Man To Steal

One day after the Detroit Tigers hit Ken Griffey Jr. with a pitch in 1990, the Seattle Mariners retaliated – hitting Cecil Fielder in the butt with a fastball. Fielder smiled and took his base.

Fielder's good nature was nearly as large as his body, which fluctuated between a listing of 240 pounds and a more NFL-lineman-like 290. No matter what the scale said, Fielder was as strong as anyone in the game. And as slow.

In the early '90s, Fielder was a force – a huge man who hit balls out of ballparks, lumbered around the bases and grinned while doing it. He was a favorite among both fans and other players, an almost impossible-to-rile spirit who coveted one statistic – stolen base.

"Mo Vaughn is ruining this game for us big men," Fielder said. "He's stealing bases and making it look easy. A lot of things would have to go right for me to get a bag. A catcher might have to faint."

In 1996, a lot of things went right twice. Fielder was credited with two stolen bases, the only ones in a career that spanned 13 seasons and 1,470 major league games. For weeks, those stolen bases were all he'd talk about.

Fielder finished his career with 319 career home runs and two steals. He still has the bag from his first stolen base.

Doug Fister: Overlooked Talent

One of the perks of my job has been hanging out on occasion with scouts, listening to what they watch for, how they determine what a 17-year-old high school kid is going to look like at 24.

The Curious Case of Doug Fister, however, reminded me not to always listen to scouts.

Yes, they're paid for making the right evaluations – and yes, they can be dead wrong. Fister proved that to me again in 2011.

When I first saw him pitch in the spring of '09, he was 6-foot-8 and about 200 pounds, a long, lean kid without an overpowering fastball. The one pitch he had that seemed capable of producing outs was a sinker.

"The kid knows how to pitch, and he may hang on as a No. 5 starter in a rotation until someone better comes along," one American League scout told me that spring. "I just think, stuff-wise, he's a little short."

That kind of thinking – and I heard the same kind of thing from two or three other scouts – colored my view of Fister.

When he didn't locate his sinker, he tended to get hammered and didn't really have another option against major league hitters.

"I think I can pitch up here," he told me that first spring. "I know I've got a lot to learn, and a lot of work to do, but I believe I can pitch here."

As a quote, Fister wasn't much help. When he went 3-4 in 10 starts in '09, I don't think he ever said anything that wasn't wrapped in caution and devoid of color.

The next season, he went 6-14 with a terrible Mariners team that routinely failed to score when he pitched – and still, what I saw in Fister was a reflection of what I'd been told by scouts.

Except somewhere in his second season, he started to convince me there was something better than a marginal big league starter. He was 26 that year, and as tough as anyone on the pitching staff.

For every loss, he took responsibility, no matter how well he'd pitched or how little his teammates scored. Seattle had two pitching coaches in '09 – Rick Adair and Carl Willis – and both loved Fister.

He kept throwing a get-it-over curve until it became something more, a pitch he could throw for a strike in any count. The velocity on that sinker crept from 88 mph to 91 mph.

Fister's control became a priority, and his walks-per-nine-innings dropped in each of his first three years.

By the spring of 2011, there were still plenty of scouts who saw Fister as a back-end-of-the-rotation pitcher. His dedication, his heart, made me think he had the chance to be more than marginal.

"Everyone on the team takes the field every day wanting to win, and my teammates want to win when I'm pitching as much as I do," Fister said. "I can't control anything but what I do out there. I don't focus on whether we're scoring runs.

"My focus is on making sure the other guys aren't scoring runs."

I wrote late in that spring that Fister would break camp as the No. 3 starter on the staff, but that no one but Felix Hernandez was pitching better.

In 21 starts for the Mariners in 2011, Fister's run support was historically low – his 'mates scored 2.33 times a game for him in a league where scoring just over four was the norm.

He went 3-11 and never once complained publicly. In visiting clubhouses, teams that faced him – and beat him – began saying good things.

"Guys were coming back to the dugout talking about his sinker, his command of it," manager Joe Maddon said after the Rays beat Fister, 3-2. "That kid is tough."

As the trading deadline approached, I knew Fister moving on was a strong possibility and wrote that.

I also talked to him in the clubhouse, told him I hoped I was wrong, but that if he were traded and left without the chance to say goodbye – a frequent occurrence – I wanted him to know just how much I admired the pitcher he'd made himself.

We shook hands and, a few days later, Fister was dealt to the Detroit Tigers for a package of players.

He made 10 starts for Detroit and went 8-1 with a 1.79 ERA.

In the post-season, he beat the New York Yankees in the decisive game of the American League Division Series, and then beat Texas in the AL Championship Series after his team had lost the first two games.

Doug Fister had become a star.

Did I know it all along? Hell, no – but I certainly changed my mind sooner than some of the men I'd so often relied upon.

Jim Fregosi: He Took It All Personally

Jim Fregosi took it all personally. As a player, he uncharacteristically booted an inning-ending ground ball and looked up to see Angels teammate Dean Chance on the mound – hands on his hips – staring at him.

"Oh, Christ," manager Bill Rigney said from the dugout.

When the third out was recorded, Chance sprinted off the mound. Fregosi was right behind him. Chance ran up the tunnel behind the dugout, into the players restroom and locked himself into a stall.

Fregosi – with Rigney hanging on his back – stormed up the same tunnel and tried to kick the door off the stall.

"Don't you ever bleeping embarrass me like that!" Fregosi screamed.

By the time he became a manager, Fregosi had mellowed a bit. He still took the game personally, along with everything that was said or done during or after each game.

Once, when he had to use left-handed pitcher Andy Hassler for an inning, knowing Hassler was gassed and had been told he wouldn't pitch, he called the pitcher into his office after the game and handed him a $100 bill.

It was Fregosi's way of saying he knew what Hassler had done was above and beyond duty.

The first spring I covered major league baseball was 1980, and Fregosi nearly killed me. I knew enough about covering beats to understand the importance of getting to know him, and when the Angels trained in Palm Springs, Fregosi had a familiar pattern.

Every night after dinner he would retire to the bar at the Gene Autry Hotel, and coaches, scouts, old friends – and writers – would join him. Every night Fregosi closed that bar, and as often as not he would retire with a bottle of Johnny Walker Black and a blonde.

After a week of this, I felt perpetually hung over. It didn't help that on my early morning drive to the ballpark, I'd see Fregosi jogging in.

Fregosi was driven and competitive, yet patient with questions if he believed you wanted an answer and not just a response. What I learned from him that first spring served me the rest of my career.

In June of the next year, I walked into a meeting between owner Gene Autry and Gene Mauch, and Autry told me he had just asked Mauch to be his new manager.

It was an exclusive story, and after the game I waited until others had left Fregosi's office before talking to him. Jim hadn't heard a thing from the front office yet. It hit him hard, and I told him if he wanted me to sit on the story a day, I'd do that.

"Write it," he said. "Do your job."

Then, rubbing a little moisture from his eyes, he extended his right hand toward me.

"Thanks for talking to me first," Fregosi said.

Freddy Garcia: Living Large And Playing Hard

Freddy Garcia came to America with a fastball born on the mounds in Venezuela and a capacity for fun that might have killed a lesser man.

At 6-foot-4, 250-pounds, Garcia was a big man on the mound.

Out on the field, he took the game seriously. Off the field, women loved him – and he loved them back. There were parties and margaritas everywhere he went, which at times made those around him shake their heads.

When he first joined the Seattle Mariners in the spring of '99, his arm was electric and so was his smile.

At 22, he had a fastball that got immediate attention, and Garcia was such an earnest kid it was impossible not to like him. The team offered him the use of a translator when dealing with the media.

Freddy gamely wanted to try handling it himself.

The first time I interviewed him, he said the key for him was 'fuk-us,' and the second time he said it, I still wasn't sure what language he was speaking.

Finally, I brought Raul Ibanez over.

"He says he has to focus on every pitch," Ibanez said after listening.

Ah. Fuk-us.

Garcia's English was always better than my Spanish, and if we went at it haltingly over the years – and 10 years later, 'focus' was still 'fuk-us' – we managed to understand one another.

His first year in the majors, Garcia won 17 games.

Two seasons later, in 2001, Garcia's slightly Mayan face earned him a nickname, Chief, and he helped lead the Mariners to the American League Championship Series.

Periodically, there were moments that made me laugh.

In an exhibition game in San Francisco, two young women showed up in the players' wives section behind home plate, wearing less than seemed possible.

They got the attention of everyone in the park, and about the time we in the press box were wondering who they were with, they each stood up and screamed "Freddy!"

One spring in Tucson, the team stayed in a hotel with a little bar attached that advertised the world's largest margarita – 46 ounces.

I met a few friends there and ordered one, sitting with my back to the wall to watch the room. I could have kept fish in a smaller glass. At the bar, Freddy was sitting in front of one.

We nodded at one another, smiled.

During the course of the next hour, I chatted with my friends and worked on my drink.

When we left for dinner, Garcia was on his third margarita. I wondered how he was still upright.

If Garcia had tried to pitch drunk, he wouldn't have been the first man in big league history to do so. If he'd pitched hung over, he'd have joined the majority.

I don't know that Freddy ever did either.

I do know his conditioning suffered after 2001, that there were times he lost focus between starts. On the mound, he didn't care less, but what he was doing off the field may have affected what he could do on it.

In 2004, when he was 4-7, the Mariners traded Garcia to

the Chicago White Sox, where manager Ozzie Guillen was a fellow Venezuelan.

Garcia felt understood in Chicago, loved Guillen and finished that season strong.

A year later, Garcia won 14 regular season games, then three more in the post-season as the White Sox won the World Series.

Injuries plagued him for years afterward, some minor, some major. After 2006, Garcia was 29-24 in his next five seasons, playing for five teams. He'd grown up, learned to appreciate what the game meant to him, and become a different kind of pitcher.

I watched Garcia in 2011 pitching with a fastball that rarely got above 90 mph, but with off-speed pitches that drove hitters crazy. In 26 starts with the New York Yankees, he won 12 games.

Garcia also made a point of going out to lunch with every young Venezuelan player he met in the game, no matter what team they were with.

"He's like family," Felix Hernandez told me. "The year I won the Cy Young Award (2010), he was one of the first people I called. He said, 'Congratulations, kid.'"

Freddy was 33 that year, but no longer felt young. His arm wasn't what it had been, and his appetites had changed. Somewhere along the way Garcia matured and was able to continue a fine career.

The smile is wiser now. Like his arm, not quite as electric, but still effective.

Kirk Gibson: If You're Not Here To Win, Then Why?

Kirk Gibson made people nervous. It was as much a part of his game as speed and power, and he had plenty of both.

On the base paths, at the plate, in the clubhouse – intimidation was second nature to him, a holdover from his football days at Michigan State.

A physical specimen when he came to Detroit in 1979, he was such a 'tools' player that the comparisons began building until there was no way he could live up to them.

Sparky Anderson said he might be the next Mickey Mantle – and Gibson thought that sounded good.

"I was a self-centered, egotistical jerk," Gibson said. "I came out of college never having had any responsibility in life, and somebody says I'm going to save the Detroit Tigers.

"I was overmatched for that situation. Nothing prepared me for it, and I brought a lot of the criticism on myself."

Over a 17-year career, Kirk Gibson never had a 30-home run season, never had 100 RBI in a season, never stole as many as 35 bases in a year.

And still, he impacted every team he played on.

Gibson helped win a World Series with the Tigers in 1984, and when the Los Angeles Dodgers signed him before the '88 season it was for more than his bat.

They wanted Gibson to make people nervous in the clubhouse.

"His reputation preceded him," Steve Sax said. "The first

day of spring training, I told him, 'You're an animal – and that's just what we need.'"

For a franchise that had grown comfortable with its Southern California image, Gibson took a place in Santa Monica, then rarely saw the ocean.

"I didn't come here to get a tan," he said.

That first spring in Los Angeles, the Dodgers talked about reaching .500. Gibson talked about winning a World Series. When Pedro Guerrero showed up late for an exhibition game, it was Gibson – not manager Tommy Lasorda – who called him on it.

"If you're not here to win, why are you here?" Gibson said. "What other reason is there to play the game?"

On the field, he loved the little aspects of the game like breaking up a double play. Off the field, the Southern California media didn't know what to make of him. Writers would approach him and Gibson would glare.

The stories that year were consistent – Kirk Gibson was a hard case, a tough interview, a borderline bad guy.

Gibson was old school with the press. If he could stare off an interviewer, fine. He wasn't here for feature stories. If you pushed past that stare and the distrust he didn't bother disguising, Gibson was expressive and thoughtful.

In the midst of leading the Dodgers to the post-season in 1988 – and sharing the National League MVP award en route – I asked Gibson about his worst year in the big leagues.

He stared at me long enough that I began to doubt he was going to answer.

"That year, 1983, was the low point for me. I hit .227 and was booed every time I showed up at the ballpark," he said quietly. "People hated me, really hated me in Detroit. By the end of the year, I didn't want to show up."

In the off-season, he got away from baseball entirely.

"I was on my horse one day, riding in the snow on top of a hill," Gibson said. "I sat looking into the wind and thought, 'You're headed in the wrong direction. You've got to quit the game or grab the bull and turn it."

Gibson turned it in Detroit. He helped the Tigers win their division, then was the MVP of his first playoff series – and hit a pair of home runs in the deciding game of the World Series.

"From the day he got here, he was a leader in the club-house," Orel Hershiser said in '88. "He showed us excuses don't cut it."

The Dodgers got the World Series that season with a less-than-formidable attack, with one dominant pitcher – Hershiser – and a roster of offensive castoffs.

Gibson got to the series injured. The Oakland Athletics got there with the Bash Brothers, with a strong-armed staff and the best closer in baseball that season, Dennis Eckersley.

Gibson had only one at-bat that Series, and beat Eckersley with a bottom-of-the-ninth inning pinch hit home run. Oakland never recovered. Los Angeles won the title.

"Kirk just did what every kid in America has done in their backyard," Mark McGwire said after the game. "No one gets to the big leagues without dreaming of hitting the home run to win a World Series game. And you know what? When he came up in that situation, he made me nervous."

Charles Gipson: He Crossed The Union Line

Charles Gipson was selected in the 63rd round of the 1991 draft, or about the time some general managers began taking their grandsons just for the fun of it.

Four years later, he was a Class A player in the Seattle Mariners spring training complex, and with the Major League Players Association on strike, teams began signing cola salesmen and biology teachers as replacement players.

Manager Lou Piniella wanted nothing to do with those men, whom he considered strike breakers. So he would, before each spring workout or game, call up one minor league player or another just to take a look at them.

One of those was Gipson, who was 23.

"The manager invited me to come up, work out and play a little," Gipson said. "At the end of the day, I'd go back to the minor league clubhouse and get dressed.

"I didn't make more money. I didn't accept a different contract or take anybody's job. The only benefit I got from it was exposure – big league coaches saw me play."

Piniella remembered the kid for his speed, his throwing arm, and his energy. In 1998, Gipson became a Mariner and played 44 major league games.

What he didn't become was a union member. The union wouldn't take him, and most of the union members never accepted him.

"Do I like the kid? Sure," veteran Jay Buhner said. "What

do I think of what he did in '95? No comment."

"Some guys have forgiven me, some never will, but I never lie about what I did or why I did it," Gipson said.

Batting coach Gerald Perry and infield coach Larry Bowa loved Gipson.

"He's dedicated, he has heart, he asks questions because he wants to learn, and he might be the best natural athlete on the team," Coach Perry said. "It's hard not to root for Charles Gipson."

Bowa tried to help Gipson, who played six positions in 1999, become a smoother infielder.

"Nobody works any harder, and he's got special speed and a great arm," Bowa said. "You hope it works out – for the team and for Charles."

Gipson spent part of five seasons in Seattle, playing in 331 games, most as a defensive replacement. He was never allowed to join the players union, never invited to dinner with a bunch of teammates headed out together.

On the field, though, he was a Mariner.

During a Dodgers-Mariners game in Los Angeles in 1999, a brawl broke out and Gipson, all 175 pounds of him, was trying to act as a peacemaker when a pair of Dodgers body-slammed him, separating a shoulder.

As Gipson lay writhing, Buhner – who was on the disabled list and not supposed to leave the Seattle bench – saw what was happening and came flying to the rescue.

He punched one player, threw another aside, then carried Gipson back to the safety of the bench.

Gipson missed two months. Buhner was suspended.

I asked Gipson one spring if he had regrets about '95.

"I wanted to play in the majors, and after a couple of years in the minors, I was nowhere," he said. "Then a big league manager asked me to show him what I could do.

"I can't go back and change it. All I can do is bust my butt and hope someday people forgive me."

By the end of his career, Gipson played parts of eight seasons and appeared in 373 games for four major league teams.

He never was allowed to join the players' union.

Dwight Gooden: One Last Chance At Glory

All the promise that was Dwight Gooden had long dimmed by May 14, 1996. No longer a starter, he'd been pushed into the New York Yankee bullpen, and off-field problems– drugs and arrests– had wasted most of his considerable talents.

On that night the Yankees were short a pitcher, so Gooden was given a start against the Seattle Mariners. And for nine innings, he reminded everyone watching what might have been.

Gooden's father was in the hospital, facing a double bypass operation the next morning. A one-time phenom who had once graced the covers of Sports Illustrated and Time magazine in the same month, Gooden had become an afterthought.

Against Seattle, the high-90s fastball of his prime was gone. So was the sharp breaking pitch that once buckled knees at the plate. What he had now was journeyman stuff and a career filled with regret.

And then he threw a no-hitter.

The Mariners got men on base all night against Gooden, using six walks, then putting two men on base in the ninth inning at Yankee Stadium with one out. Facing hitters like Alex Rodriguez, Ken Griffey Jr. and Edgar Martinez, Gooden was clearly exhausted by the eighth inning.

Just as clearly, he wanted to stay in the game.

Manager Joe Torre watched him throw 100 pitches, then slide past 110 pitches, past 120.

Gassed, Gooden let the Mariners put the tying run on second base with one out when he wild-pitched trying to overthrow a breaking pitch.

It was a game and an inning that would later be the basis for a Kevin Costner film, but this was reality. Dwight Gooden was 32 and all but out of pitches. He hadn't had a winning season in five years, hadn't pitched in the majors at all a year earlier.

"I was out of chances, I was out of the game," Gooden said. "The Yankees were the only team that gave me another chance."

Gooden struck out Buhner for the second out in the ninth inning as his pitch count pushed past 130. On his 135th pitch of the night, he struck out Paul Sorrento and earned the seventh no-hitter in Yankee history.

"He beat us with guts," Griffey said afterward. "He didn't have an overpowering pitch, he just kept hitting his spots with that slow curve, changing speeds.

"I don't know what he was like at his best, but he pitched tonight. We knew what was coming and it didn't matter."

I saw Gooden at his best, in the '80s when he dominated the game and won 91 times before turning 25. He looked immortal, and thought he was.

Life taught him otherwise. Cocaine humbled him, all but ruined him, and a Hall of Fame career flamed out.

On May 14, 1996, I didn't see the immortal Gooden. Instead, I saw a mortal use whatever was left in him to reach for greatness. It was impossible not to share in his genuine joy.

Rich Gossage: An Intimidating Presence

How important was the role of closer when Rich Gossage was breaking in? In 1975, The Goose won nine games – and saved 26 with a 1.84 ERA – for the Chicago White Sox.

The next year, they made him a starting pitcher.

Gossage only had as many as 30 saves in a season twice in his 22-year major league career, yet he was as classic a closer as anyone in history.

The glare. The intensity. The fastball.

When Gossage entered the game, no one wondered what pitch he might be featuring that day. And if the fastball got away a bit, say up and in, then that was your problem, not his.

"He was a competitor who beat you with a pitch you knew was coming," Graig Nettles said. "If you hit it out, he was mad – but at himself, not you. And when he beat you, it was by putting a pitch where you didn't want it."

As the Yankees' closer in the late '70s and early '80s, Gossage seemed more like a fictional character than a right-handed relief pitcher.

During games, he rarely took the field before the fifth or sixth inning, choosing instead to remain in the clubhouse. Was he studying hitters on television, watching how his pitchers were working the other team?

As often as not, he was asleep.

On or off the field, The Goose offered a menacing presence. When Ken Griffey was a Yankees teammate, his son – Ken Griffey Jr. – often roamed the clubhouse. Junior was terrified of Gossage.

"He'd lay there with a newspaper over his face, and we were never sure if he was alive under there," Griffey would say years later. "When he'd sit up, he'd have that look ..."

Major league hitters knew it well.

Late in his career, Gossage no longer owned the ninth inning. The last five seasons he pitched, he never saved more than four games.

"I play for that one inning, facing hitters when it matters," Gossage said in his last year. "Now, it may be the sixth inning, not the ninth. But games are won and lost in the sixth inning, too."

Gossage wasn't what he had been for so long in those final years. Ask him to mop up a one-sided game, he was likely to get pounded. But give him the ball in a jam, The Goose looked the same on the mound.

On one of the many nights a Seattle starter didn't have much in 1994, Gossage was called into the game in the fifth inning with the bases loaded and no one out.

He struck out the side, pumped a fist into his glove and trotted off the field.

"You know why he was so good out there?" Lou Piniella said. "Sometimes, he was just tougher than the other guy. He couldn't stand losing. With the game on the line, Goose was just tougher."

Ken Griffey Sr.: Quick to Anger

Early in his career, Ken Griffey Jr. decided to talk about a teenage cry for help – his consuming a bottle of aspirin and winding up in the hospital, all because of a breakup with a girlfriend. It was Junior's way of trying to help other kids.

Ken Griffey Sr. was incensed when he heard about the interview, and as I was walking to my car in the parking lot he skidded his car to a stop and began berating me.

"You're taking advantage of the kid and his good nature," Senior told me. "You have no right to write about it. I'm taking this personally, I promise you."

Before he pulled away, I managed to tell Griffey that I wasn't the writer involved. This wasn't to pass the buck – the story just wasn't mine, it belonged to a fellow beat writer, Bob Finnigan.

Senior pondered that for a moment and then sped off. He never spoke another word about that story to me. And Junior never had a problem with Finnigan writing it.

At the end of the 1990 season, the two Griffeys had played together, the first father-and-son tandem in major league history. Junior played center, Senior was in left field, and the final month of the year in Seattle was magical.

There were moments that month that may never be repeated: back-to-back home runs by father and son, Senior standing under a lazy fly ball only to have Junior race past at the last moment and steal it from him – and so many laughs and hugs in the dugout.

There was also a long walk back to the team hotel one night with Senior and me. On it, Griffey talked about the father who'd left him and his family when he was two-years-old and about the lifetime of wondering what he'd done wrong at such a young age.

For a man with such a marvelous major league career, there was a lot of anger in Griffey Sr. More than 20 years after a World Series 'slight,' he still talked of manager Sparky Anderson only as a man who'd embarrassed him in what might have been the finest hour of his career.

In the mid-90s, after he'd retired and moved on to other baseball jobs, I ran into Senior outside the Mariners spring clubhouse and we exchanged pleasantries. I asked why he wasn't in the clubhouse, and he stunned me with an angry diatribe about Lou Piniella, who he felt had given him less than proper respect at some point in their careers.

Because I liked both men, I told Piniella of the encounter and Piniella found Senior and within 20 minutes the two were embracing. I never pursued it further. It was their story, not mine.

I have no doubt, however, that much of Senior's response to slights, perceived or otherwise, went back to the father he'd never known. As he grew up, a child on welfare, he'd vowed no one would disrespect him or his family that way again.

That one night walking back to the hotel, Senior opened up in the dark about the pain and shame his father had caused him, about wounds he could never quite close. Before the walk ended, he was wiping at his eyes and so was I.

I never held anything Senior said against him after that. To me, he had some anger coming.

Ken Griffey Jr.: Couldn't Forgive A Slight

When anyone found out what I did for a living, the first two questions they asked rarely varied – who was the best player I'd ever seen play and which one was my favorite.

Most of my career, the answer to both was the same: Ken Griffey Jr.

My first interview with him came before his 19th birthday, when he worried about dealing with the 'setbacks' he was sure to experience in professional baseball.

What kind of setbacks, I asked.

"You know, like making outs," he said, dead serious.

Junior had once played an entire Little League season, not making an out until the final day. That, of course, was a setback.

That first spring with the Seattle Mariners, Griffey was funny and maddening, candid and childlike and occasionally childish. Twenty years later, he was much the same.

My God, he could make me laugh.

What he also did, from 1989 on, was play baseball as well as anyone on the planet, and that wasn't just my opinion. In a vote of his peers – 750 major league players – Griffey was voted Player of the Decade for the '90s.

All of us covering Junior felt at times like Dutch uncles. Once he called me from his Arizona hotel room at midnight, asked me to come up. I did, and saw he'd been crying.

A business magazine in Seattle had printed an article about Griffey's salary, and how he clearly cared more about money than baseball.

Junior wanted to know how someone he'd never met or spoken to could write something so hurtful.

We talked it out that night, with me finally telling him there would be, sadly, worse things written about him in his career. He said he didn't know if he could bear reading them.

As it turned out, we were both right.

As he became the first superstar in Seattle history, Griffey's personality became clearer off the field.

"I love kids," he told me once. "It's adults I have trouble with."

Baseball's partnership with the Make A Wish Foundation often brought kids with grim futures to ballparks around the league, and no one was better with them than Griffey.

He wouldn't just talk to them, he would play with them – on their level.

Once in Chicago, a dying boy was brought to the park an hour before game time to meet Frank Thomas, who'd been told the boy was coming earlier.

Thomas couldn't break free. The boy was devastated, the White Sox public relations staff was helpless. Then someone thought of Griffey.

Junior came out, took the kid into the Mariners clubhouse and talked to him until game time. When the boy left, he was wearing a Griffey cap – backwards, of course – wielding a Griffey bat, his wrists strengthened with Junior's sweat bands.

Griffey never stopped talking unless he was playing baseball. He would talk to friends on the telephone, talk to teammates and coaches in the clubhouse and, when all else failed, talk to writers.

He made a point of finding our 'weak spots,' as he called them. How many kids we had, how he could best torment us.

Griffey once offered $500 to a rookie teammate to shave his head.

When I laughed at that, he offered me a thousand to shave my beard and my head.

"You don't have enough money to get me to do that," I told him.

Griffey grinned.

"Oh, yes I do," he said.

Fortunately, he didn't pursue it.

What was Griffey like? When he first met outfielder Patrick Lennon in the minor leagues, the two almost came to blows. A few years later, as Junior's star was ascending, Lennon wound up in jail for months.

Only one man visited Lennon behind bars – Griffey.

"He was the last guy on earth I'd have figured cared," Lennon said. "And it turned out he was the only one who did."

The kicker? The next spring, after talking to Lennon, then Junior, I set up a photographer to take a photo of them together before a workout after each signed off on the idea.

The morning came, the photographer arrived and was waiting on the infield. Lennon was ready. Griffey said he wasn't taking the shot.

I asked nicely. No deal.

I pleaded my case as a professional. He didn't budge.

Finally, I snapped.

"Goddamn it, Junior, fine – don't take the bleeping photo, be an ass ..."

At which point Ken leaped up from his stool, beaming.

"OK, let's go," he said. "I was just wondering how long you'd go before you got really pissed off."

We took the photo. I'd rarely seen Griffey happier.

When we were both staying in the team hotel in Palm

Springs, Junior met my daughter as we were walking out of the room one evening and chatted with her like an old friend.

She was 12 and had a crush on him.

"What kind of car do you want when you turn 16?" he asked.

"Whatever you drive," she said.

Griffey, who had a Porsche loaded with toys, looked up at me.

"You're in big trouble, dad," he said.

For years, each spring, Griffey would do a sit-down interview with me and my best friend in the business, Arizona sportswriter Lloyd Herberg. In the spring of '95, Lloyd was dying of cancer but still trying to work.

He could no longer drive, so I drove him to camp, and we walked into the clubhouse together. Lloyd was pale and shaky, clearly not well.

Junior, who noticed everything that happened in his clubhouse, waved me over and asked me what was wrong with my friend. I told him.

"Bring him over," he said.

I did, and Junior made Lloyd take the stool beside his, and then turned to me.

"Get lost," he said.

I did, and the two talked for more than an hour, only sometimes about baseball. Later that summer, Lloyd died, and did so thinking Ken Griffey Jr. was a good and decent man, far more complex than most of our peers made him out to be.

I never disagreed.

I covered Junior throughout his Seattle years, interviewed him a half dozen times when he was with the Reds, then with the White Sox. Once, in the Cincinnati clubhouse, he pointed me out to teammates.

"See those gray hairs?" he asked. "He likes to say his daughter gave them to him, but I did it."

Junior made a triumphant return to Seattle in 2009, and our relationship hadn't changed. He still loved nothing more than torturing teammates and, in a pinch, beat writers.

I never covered a man I was fonder of.

By May, 2010, the Mariners were a team in disarray – by year's end, their manager and coaching staff would be fired, their roster almost completely turned over.

Junior wasn't hitting and wasn't playing, which meant he wasn't happy. I talked to a club official who said the Mariners were trying to find a way to part ways, respectfully, with the best player in franchise history.

I was doing a story on that, saying in an unposted blog entry that it appeared Griffey's situation might come to a head by June 1. Then, in the clubhouse, a veteran player called me over.

Griffey, he said, hadn't been called upon to pinch hit in the eighth inning of a game that week because he'd been in the clubhouse asleep in the seventh.

Sadly, it fit with what I'd already written. Junior had lost the drive, all but lost interest in games he wasn't playing. Still ... sleeping in the clubhouse during games?

I asked a second player, one I'd known for several years, and he confirmed Griffey had been asleep.

On a Monday morning at Sea-Tac airport, I folded that information into the blog I'd written, choosing to downplay it by waiting until well into the story before mentioning it.

All it needed before I submitted it was a comment from Junior, which I intended to get late that afternoon in Baltimore. I clicked 'save' on the blog, or meant to.

What I clicked was 'publish.'

There was nothing inaccurate in the post, nothing I'd have

rewritten or changed – but I didn't yet have Junior's side.

When I arrived in Baltimore close to six hours later, my cell phone had more than 100 missed calls and messages. The story was on my blog, and the blog had gone viral.

On June 2, Griffey retired from the game – doing so in a telephone call to the Mariners team president, made from the road as Junior drove away.

We never spoke again.

Harold Reynolds, a good man who liked us both, tried to reconnect me with Junior, have us talk it out. It didn't work. I'd call Junior, get his answering machine, leave a message.

Nothing.

I don't blame him. When I'd told him 20 years earlier that someone would write something worse about him than that he liked money more than baseball, I'd never dreamed it would be me.

The story was accurate.

It broke both our hearts.

Vladimir Guerrero: High Or Low, He Hit Them All

After spending seven years in obscurity with the Montreal Expos, Vladimir Guerrero brought his act to America in 2004 but remained an enigma.

A Dominican-born player who not only swung at nearly everything but also usually hit it, Guerrero never trusted his English in interviews or conversations with the media.

He was good-natured, almost sweet in trying to answer questions through an interpreter, but what if he'd been able to speak more freely?

Vlad might have been an even bigger star than his abilities made him.

Pitchers studied him and looked for a weakness.

"You can make him chase the fastball," Felix Hernandez said, "but you'd better not make a mistake. Vlad hits mistakes a long way."

Ryan Franklin once got ahead in the count and threw a split-fingered fastball to Guerrero, and the ball broke down toward the dirt and arrived about ankle high.

Guerrero hit it out to straightaway center field.

"That's not right," Franklin said, watching the video replay over and over. "You can't be behind in the count and hit *that* pitch *that* far."

I once asked Guerrero if he sat on certain pitches, guessed what pitch was coming, and he started shaking his head even before I finished.

"I look fastball, I look for the spin of the ball, but I can hit any pitch hard if I see it good," he said through an interpreter. "I like the ball up, I like the ball down ..."

When he laughed, it was the sound of joy. Guerrero loved hitting, and running – and did one well.

Over the years, Guerrero's exuberant base-running would drive his managers – like the Angels Mike Scioscia – half out of their minds. Guerrero's knees left him with average speed, but he had the instincts of someone much faster.

So he was thrown out a lot.

"Vladdy will round a base and everyone in his dugout will be thinking 'Stop now, just stop' and he'll keep going," one American League scout told me over lunch. "It's as if something in him forces him to try to take one more base."

Guerrero played the game with a child's innocence and genuinely enjoyed talking and laughing with teammates and opposing players. Pitchers tended to avoid him.

"He's an animal at the plate," Jarrod Washburn once told me. "I mean that with respect, but mortal players can't hit good pitches the way he does. He'll hit them off his shoe tops and eye-high and absolutely crush them.

"If I get ahead of him, I've thrown the ball right down the middle to him – hey, that pitch surprises him."

Guerrero drove in 100 RBI in a season 10 times and was the American League Most Valuable Player his first season out of Montreal.

Some great hitters are feared for their discipline, their ability to hit with two strikes. Vlad was a different kind of fearsome – totally undisciplined, he might swing at anything.

"I've thrown him my best pitch down, away, in and up and it didn't matter," Washburn said. "If he's hot, he can hit anything. If he's cold, you can get away with anything, but when he's hot you want to just walk him."

Washburn wasn't joking. Five times Guerrero led the

league in intentional walks and, in a career still going in 2011, he'd been intentionally put on first base 250 times.

For good reason.

Allowed to swing the bat, over all or part of 16 seasons, Guerrero averaged 34 home runs and 113 RBI.

The only pitches safe from him were those he couldn't reach.

Tony Gwynn: A Heavy Weight At Bat

Noon is ugly in Yuma, Arizona. Seven hours before a Padres spring training game, the only two people in the San Diego complex were the clubhouse attendant and me.

I was thinking I'd been set up. That Tony Gwynn had told me to meet him here at noon and was somewhere air-conditioned now, laughing.

And then down the sizzling asphalt drive came Gwynn, riding a bicycle, waving like we were old friends.

"You thought I'd stiffed you, didn't you?" he said.

Well ...

No one but Gwynn would show up this early for a meaningless spring game, but to his way of thinking it was just another day at the office. Spend an hour watching video, an hour alone in the batting cage with a pitching machine, a short break, and then 30 minutes with a coach throwing to him.

Gwynn may have known his swing better than any hitter in the game. Show him a videotape of one swing – just one – and he could identify the year in which it was made. Nothing about his .338 lifetime average was accidental.

"All I hear about is my weight and my natural ability," Gwynn said. "I got a fan letter the year I hit .394 from a guy who had a picture of me playing basketball in college. You know what he wrote? He said, 'You were fat then, too.'"

Gwynn had one of the most delightful laughs in baseball, a high-pitched giggle he rarely tried to suppress.

"You can't win in this game. Pitchers talk about facing me and say they might as well throw it down the middle – but they never do," Gwynn said.

"It's March, the games don't matter, but in 6 ½ hours I'll be facing Randy Johnson. And I guarantee the shit he throws me will be supersonic and not down the middle."

Nothing stopped Gwynn's hitting. Not injuries and not off-the-field maladies.

In 1987, investments made for him by an agent and advisers collapsed, and Gwynn declared bankruptcy.

He batted .370.

In 1993, he played the second half on a knee so badly damaged it required surgery the day after the season ended.

He batted .358.

And in '94, he lost his father, with whom he shared every good moment in his career.

Gwynn hit .394 that year.

Writers were tougher on him than pitchers. He never batted less than .300 in a season. Never failed to show up for a scheduled interview. And never, he insisted, caught a break from the media.

"I think you guys have written my weight as often as you have my batting average," he said. "Well, my body was always soft – but I got quite a bit out of this body. People wrote about my weight after my first batting title, and they wrote about it after my seventh."

Bill Haselman: Beaned By A Girl

Bill Haselman was every inch a major league catcher – strong, durable, and capable of absorbing all the pain the position required.

For 13 seasons, he was a backup catcher, never playing more than 77 games in a year, working for four big league teams, two of them twice. He worked well with pitchers, played hard when given the chance and was a man others liked being around.

Haselman enjoyed every day he spent in uniform and there was nothing he wouldn't do if asked. So, it wasn't unusual when a team had a high-profile guest throwing out the ceremonial first pitch that Haselman would be behind the plate.

Those moments were routine. Catch the ball, trot to the mound, shake hands, pose for a photo, sign the baseball and then head back to the dugout.

One evening in Seattle, the Mariners were honoring the University of Washington's women's softball team, which had won a championship. Their top pitcher was going to throw out the first pitch – but with a softball, which was considerably larger than a baseball.

Haselman was asked to catch that first pitch and hunkered down behind home plate.

The woman pitcher came down off the mound, and walked to about the distance of a softball mound. Haselman expected her to throw him a slow-pitch softball delivery.

She threw him a rising fastball.

"I knew I was in trouble when she started a windup that was full speed," Haselman said later. "I had no idea what was coming."

With a crowd settled in the Kingdome seats watching, that pitch hit the top of Haselman's glove, then the top of his head, sending his cap several feel in the air.

Haselman went down like a turtle on its back, stunned – and the Mariners dugout exploded with laughter.

The catcher got slowly to his feet, retrieved his cap and the softball and met the woman in the infield. Grinning, he posed for the obligatory photo, signed the ball and walked to the dugout.

Teammates had tears in their eyes they'd laughed so hard.

Years later, when he was with Boston, I asked Haselman about the experience, whether he remembered it.

"She almost killed me," he said, laughing. "That ball could just as easily have hit me between the eyes. I don't think anyone who saw it ever had another memory of me other than that one."

Over the years, the amicable Haselman would be asked to catch a similar first pitch, and he always agreed. But he did one thing differently than he had that night in the Kingdome.

Haselman always wore a catcher's mask for ceremonial first pitches.

Sterling Hitchcock: Keeping It Real

All Sterling Hitchcock needed to know about the New York media he learned after starting a September game for the Yankees in 1992 against the Kansas City Royals.

"I allowed one hit and hit a batter – George Brett," Hitchcock said. "Afterward, all the writers asked me what it was like facing Brett, and I said I'd tried to look at him as just another hitter.

"If I hadn't, how could I have pitched to him? I mean, I knew who he was."

Years later, Hitchcock remembered the stories that followed that first start.

"One headline was 'Brett Just Another Hitter," he said, and laughed.

A small-town kid who came to professional baseball straight out of high school, Hitchcock was a New York Yankee at 21 and a Seattle Mariner at 25.

He understood how strange a trip he was on.

"By the time I was in my fifth big league season, I'd played with four Cy Young Award winners, two batting champions and the best player in baseball – Ken Griffey Jr.," Hitchcock said.

I asked if there were times he had trouble believing it all.

"Most of the time," he answered with a laugh.

Hitchcock was delightfully candid about his career and life. When I first talked to him about the trade to Seattle, he started his answer by telling me about his wife, Carrey.

"My wife liked New York, but it can be intimidating," he said. "We met in junior high in Brandon, Florida, and it only has about three stop lights. She was afraid to drive in New York.

"When the Yankees called to say I'd been traded, I hung up and told her, 'It's Seattle' – and she actually did a couple of cartwheels."

At one point with the Mariners, Hitchcock had trouble getting through the middle innings of games he started, a stretch that frustrated him.

Griffey, who teased everybody in the Seattle clubhouse, got on Hitchcock one day in Anaheim – in typical Junior fashion.

"In the first inning, you've got cannon balls," Griffey said, not talking about Hitchcock's pitches. "By the fourth inning, you've got softballs. And in the sixth inning ..."

Everyone in the clubhouse, including Hitchcock, waited for it ...

"Canary balls!" Junior yelled.

The room broke up, and no one laughed harder than Hitchcock, who was tougher than most knew. In his one year with Seattle, he won 13 games.

Traded to San Diego the next winter, Hitchcock made me laugh with his reaction.

"New York, Seattle, San Diego – what I need now is a trade to the Florida Marlins and I'll have all points of the compass covered," he said.

Hitchcock's toughness was proven in '98 when he was the National League Championship Series MVP while pitching for the Padres and went 3-1 with a 1.23 earned run average in the post-season.

Three years later, he won the fifth game of the 2001 World

Series game pitching for the Yankees.

When he retired after the 2004 season, Hitchcock went back to the classroom and became a certified personal trainer. He and Carrey settled in Naples, Fla.

It had more than three stop lights, but it wasn't New York.

Frank Howard: He Called, And They Came

The first time I saw Frank Howard in person, he was emerging naked from a sauna, carrying a pair of 40-pound dumbbells, and sweating profusely. His body was chiseled, his stature a bit daunting.

He was 54 -years-old.

Imagine the man in his prime, all 6-foot-7, 255 pounds of him at the plate. In 16 major league seasons, he hit 382 home runs and caused more third basemen to play deep than any player of his generation.

Jim Slaton remembers the first time he faced Howard, who by then was at the end of his career.

"Our third baseman trotted to the mound, picked up the resin bag and said 'Pitch this guy away,'" Slaton said. "Frank walked up to the plate, got in the box and just looked at me. He was the biggest player I'd ever seen."

Then Howard did something Slaton never forgot.

"He leaned forward just a bit, and tapped the outside line of the other batters' box with his bat," Slaton said. "And I'm thinking, 'I'm supposed to pitch this guy outside?'"

There was no 'outside' with Howard at the plate, and few men ever hit a ball harder. One of the strongest players in the game, Howard was a subject of discussion in every other clubhouse early in his career – opposing players wondered what to do with him in case of a brawl.

In 1,895 games, Frank Howard never charged the mound

during an at-bat. When the bench emptied, he was there, sorting players out in his own way.

"Frank would kind of wade into the pile, grab an opposing player, pick him up and throw him," Ron Fairly said. "And he could throw you a long way. He was never angry when he did it. There's no telling how far he could have thrown you if he was mad."

As a coach, Howard remained his own man. He wouldn't pack a bag for a trip – just wear one outfit, every day. When he got to the ballpark, he'd take it off and have it washed, then put it back on after the game.

And he smoked cigars the size of fungo bats.

"If you get off the hotel elevator and smell cigar smoke, you know you're on Hondo's floor," Alvin Davis said.

In the spring of his 55th year, Howard was coaching the Mariners on one of the team's three practice fields. An airhorn used to signal field changes or summon the team together malfunctioned.

No problem. Howard simply bellowed. Players across the complex heard him and came running.

Brian Hunter: He Owed His Speed To His Sister

Growing up, Brian Hunter never considered himself fast. Not when his older brother could out-run him. Not when his older sister could out-run them both.

So he played baseball because he could hit and field, and when the Houston Astros drafted him, Hunter believed it was for those reasons, not his speed.

The truth was, Hunter not only wasn't fast – when he tried to be, he fell down. A lot.

"My first year in pro ball, I'd get a hit and light out for first base and fall down before I got there," Hunter said. "It happened all the time. They started calling me 'Bambi' because I had long arms and legs and didn't have a clue how to use them."

The first off-season, he called in a specialist, a world-class sprinter from the University of Oregon. It was his sister. After talking to Hunter, I called her. When I mentioned what Hunter had told me, she started laughing.

"Brian was always quick, but his form was so rotten he looked clumsy," Stefanie Hunter-Haroldson said. "He'd come out of the batter's box all bent at the waist, leaning so far forward he was off-balance.

"Someone told him he should run all the way to first base like he was coming out of the starting blocks. His arms looked like he was boxing. His stride was way too long."

She hesitated, then laughed again.

"He did fall down a lot. And the funny thing is, he looked worse running than I'm making it sound."

Going to his sister that first fall was the smartest thing Hunter could have done.

"She made me faster," he said. "That changed my career."

Hunter-Haroldson treated her younger brother like a beginning runner which, in essence, he was.

"I had him bring his arms in, got him more balanced," she said. "We did a lot of drills, working on a quick first step, on balance, on stride. We worked out three times a week together."

Then the unexpected happened.

"All our lives, whenever we'd run, I'd beat Brian," she said. "That fall, all of a sudden he beat me. Then he started crushing me. I mean, he'd never been close and I'd run against world-class sprinters. All of a sudden, he was fast."

When the Houston Astros brought Hunter to the big leagues, it wasn't just for his bat and glove.

"My first at-bat, I singled," Hunter said. "On the second pitch, I stole second base. I spent years in the minor leagues, and there's no question that what got me to the majors was my speed.

"It's what I have, it's my game, and it makes me a factor offensively, helps me on defense. Speed gave me a career in the majors."

It was a 10-year career, and during it Brian Hunter ran well enough to lead the American League in stolen bases in 1997, stealing 74 times. Three times, he was paid more than a million dollars a year.

And not once in the 1,000 major league games he played did Brian Hunter ever fall down on his way to first base.

Butch Huskey: Not Too Big For The Big League

For every young player told he's too small to play major league baseball there's a Butch Huskey, who was told he was too big.

Huskey couldn't deny his size – 6-foot-3 and anywhere from 245 to 275 pounds. But he had a stock answer to anyone who doubted his ability to play.

"Sometimes, people only see the outside of you," Huskey told me. "They can't see your heart. There are small people in the big leagues, and it's for one reason. They have big hearts.

"I have a big heart, too."

The son of a strict Oklahoma policeman, Huskey collected Beanie Babies as he worked his way through the New York Mets farm system. Huskey came up with the Mets, who turned the third baseman into an outfielder in mid-season one year, then moved him to first base when he struggled. Wherever they put him, Huskey hustled — and hit baseballs a long way.

Fifteen home runs in 1996, 24 more in '97. Huskey played all-out, the way his father had demanded. But the Mets had plenty of outfielders. They traded Huskey to Seattle in the winter of 1998.

Playing left field for the Mariners one day in 1999, Huskey was captured on tape in a video that went viral and can still be found on the internet today.

On a ball hit well out of the park, Huskey was in pursuit when the left field wall in Minnesota's Metrodome interrupted him. Huskey hit that wall in full stride - the 'boom' that followed was audible throughout the 'domed ball park.

"Once we knew Butch wasn't hurt, people started giggling," Twins outfielder Jacque Jones said. "I mean, both teams – everybody. No one had ever seen a full-speed face plant like that."

The next day in batting practice, Huskey took the field to find someone had chalked in a body outline on the left field wall. Players from both teams teased him, then hugged him.

Huskey had a big heart and loved the attention of his Seattle teammates. In 119 games with the Mariners, he batted .290 with 15 home runs and 49 RBI.

That July, as the trading deadline neared, the Mariners sent Huskey to Boston and a pennant race. The deal broke his heart. Huskey missed teammates Ken Griffey Jr. and Jay Buhner, and manager Lou Piniella.

One year and three teams later, Huskey was done. After parts of seven seasons, his baseball career was over.

Huskey was still huge, could still hit the ball a long way. That big heart just wasn't in it anymore.

Ichiro: Zen Meets Baseball

In Japan, where he played nine seasons, Ichiro Suzuki was more recognized than the prime minister, but then no politician had won seven batting titles and three Most Valuable Player Awards.

When he was declared an international free agent, the Seattle Mariners bid $13 million for the rights to talk to him, then signed him for three years and another $18 million.

His first season in major league baseball, he was allowed to use only his first name on the back of his jersey – something no other player had ever been allowed to do.

Then he won a batting title, the Rookie of the Year Award *and* the American League Most Valuable Player in his first season.

Early on, Ichiro was both eccentric and charming, a sort of zen-meets-baseball experience.

"The first few weeks in spring training, I'd been told about his power, that he could bat third, and then all I saw were soft line drives to the opposite field," his first manager Lou Piniella said.

"Finally, the games started, and after three games, he still hadn't hit a ball to the right side of the field. I got a little worried."

In Piniella's quiet way, he approached Ichiro.

He said, "God Almighty, son, can you just show me that you can pull the ball?"

Ichiro pulled the ball – hit a long home run beyond the fence in right field and a second over a barbeque stand. Piniella backed off.

"The biggest adjustment is that in Japan, the tempo of every pitcher was like 1-2 and 3," Ichiro explained to me. "Here, it's more like 1-2-3, with no 'and' between 2 and 3.

"I had to take the 'and' out of my swing to match that tempo. I did it by changing the stride with my front foot."

How much of a change? Ichiro held his thumb and forefinger an inch apart.

The first spring in America, Ichiro was followed by a few dozen Japanese writers and television crews. Not only was he the first Japanese position player to sign in the big leagues, he was a Japanese superstar.

Japanese publications called Seattle writers and asked them to freelance stories – paying them not with checks but with hand-delivered currency.

Ichiro wasn't pleased with that. What he told Japanese reporters was not always what he told American writers. I told him I'd turned down offers from Japan, and that he would only read what I wrote about him in my paper or through American wire services.

He bowed in respect. I did the same.

Ichiro was a huge fan of the game, and in that initial season, he was thrilled to meet players he had only read about – George Brett, Kirby Puckett, Larry Walker and the retired Hall of Famer Ernie Banks, who showed up in Chicago just to meet him.

And then late in September, with the Mariners having wrapped up a division title, Ichiro was leading the AL batting race. I asked if he wanted to win that title, too.

He shook his head 'no.'

"If I allow myself to get caught up in that, what becomes

important? I would be hoping for other players to make more outs, but if they did, would it make me a better hitter?" he asked.

"If you have the ability to hit .350 but hit .320 and win a batting title, is that an achievement?

"A .250 hitter who uses 100 percent of his ability should be more fulfilled than a player hitting .350 using 80 percent of his ability," Ichiro said. "My fulfillment will come when I play to the best of my ability."

Ichiro hit .350 that year and won a batting title. Three years later, he batted .372 and won another.

Throughout his career in Seattle, Ichiro clearly was unique, which didn't always endear him to teammates. Though he spoke English fairly well, he always used a translator to deal with the media.

He had a masseuse travel with the team, kept his bats not in a bag like everyone else – but instead in a dehumidified case. Ichiro's style in clothes was legendary.

"About half the outfits he wears, I'd like to burn," said reliever Eddie Guardado, a notorious practical joker. "One day he's going to come off the field and find a pile of ashes near his locker and have to go home in his underwear."

While most players respected him, there were those who believed Ichiro wasn't a great teammate. From Ichiro's perspective, what he wanted from teammates was respect, not friendship.

That changed in 2009 – when the Mariners signed aging free agent Ken Griffey Jr., the first superstar in franchise history.

Weeks into the season, I walked into the Seattle clubhouse and saw something I'd never seen. Ichiro was on the ground, giggling in childlike delight-and-rage as Griffey tickled him.

"Now say, 'Black is beautiful' and I'll stop," Junior said.

"Black is beautiful!" Ichiro screamed, and Griffey stopped.

Ichiro was beaming. This, I had to follow up. I asked Ichiro about Griffey.

"He's the only teammate I would ever let do that," Ichiro said. "In Japan, all relationships are respectful, so no one would ever do that to me.

"If someone else did it here, I'd probably punch them in the mouth."

So why Junior?

"I always thought that opening up in baseball would be close to impossible with so many differences between me and the other players," he said. "It's been close to a miracle with Junior.

"We have a special relationship – something I've never had before.

"He's changed the way I sense things. I thought time would be the biggest factor in building a friendship. Junior did it from the first day," Ichiro said.

I asked Griffey how it had happened.

"Here's why we became friends. I don't want anything from him, he doesn't want anything from me, except friendship," Griffey said. "There are no ulterior motives, no hidden agendas. I just want to be his friend."

It was the happiest we'd seen Ichiro since 2001.

A year later in 2010, Griffey retired in mid-season, and a story I wrote played a small part in that. Junior never forgave me.

Ichiro, his friend, never spoke to me one-on-one again.

In 2011, he had his worst professional season, batting .272. I wanted to ask him about what he'd said in '01, and whether at .272 he'd used all his ability that season.

That was his choice, my loss. And no one replaced Griffey for either one of us.

Bo Jackson: In An Elite World, He Was Special

Jim Lefebvre had a standing rule in the Kingdome whenever the Kansas City Royals came to Seattle – Mariners pitchers were not allowed to watch Bo Jackson take batting practice.

Catcher Scott Bradley watched in their place and actually moaned whenever Jackson made solid contact.

Bo would stand beside the batting cage talking to teammates or opposing players until his round came up, then hop in and take his swings. Sometimes he used his bat. Sometimes, he'd just grab one on the way in, not caring whose it was.

Either way, no one ever hit a baseball farther. Jackson reached the upper deck in straightaway center field at the Kingdome.

"I've played here for years," Bradley said after watching that one. "No one else in the league has ever come within 50 feet of that."

The game has always featured great athletes, but even at that elite level, Jackson was special, and everyone who played with or against him realized it. He could run faster, hit harder and throw farther than anyone around him.

And players loved him.

Seattle Mariner Harold Reynolds tried to score from first base one night on a double into the left field corner in the 'dome. As he got to third base, Jackson was just getting to the ball on the warning track. Reynolds headed for the plate.

Jackson picked up the ball, straightened and threw flat-footed—without a bit of momentum—and his throw beat Reynolds to the plate by 10 feet.

Reynolds turned and stared at Jackson, who tipped his cap and smiled.

Years after he retired, Jackson showed up in Tucson one spring and stood around the cage talking to players from the Mariners and the Diamondbacks.

As he chatted, Mariner outfielder Mike Cameron spied him from across the field, sprinted over and leaped upon Jackson's back. Jackson didn't so much as sway with the impact, seemed not to have noticed Cameron had landed upon him.

He finished his conversation and then turned his head slightly toward Cameron.

"Somebody get this little pest off me," Jackson said.

Everyone around was relieved when he smiled.

Reggie Jackson: Ego And Magic

There were four or five Reggie Jacksons, and I got to meet all of them in the years we were together with the California Angels.

Reggie the humble. The Raging Reggie, a cold, cruel version of Reggie. The articulate, thoughtful Reggie. There were times one or the other would instantly appear, bumping another Reggie aside – and I don't believe he completely controlled the transformations.

I learned covering Reggie that about once a year, he would go off on every beat writer covering the team, usually without reason. It was his way of showing teammates he wasn't the media darling some thought he was. It was also his way of keeping writers in their place.

I walked into a cramped Boston visiting clubhouse one afternoon, and from a far corner Reggie stood up and began screaming about a "treacherous motherfucking son of a bitch."

I smiled, because Reggie was always high theater at such moments, and I was curious to see who he was raging at this time.

It was me.

He went on at some length about how he couldn't trust me and that I was a degenerate, never quite explaining why. I hadn't written a word about him recently – certainly nothing critical – but perhaps that was what this was about.

Having told the world my flaws, Reggie sat down. We

avoided each other that afternoon.

The next day, on the field before batting practice, he called me by my nickname, 'Lash,' and quietly – with few teammates around – said he'd just been blowing off steam. It wasn't quite an apology, because Reggie didn't apologize. But we got along fine thereafter.

The year Jackson came to the Angels as a free agent after leaving the New York Yankees, he batted .188 in April with one home run. When the Angels went to Yankee Stadium late that month, the tabloids were running 'Reggie Watches.'

He hadn't hit a home run, yet. The implications were that he was done, that Yankee owner George Steinbrenner had made a brilliant decision in not pursuing Jackson.

Reggie was in such demand before the first game of the series that the Yankees set aside an interview room for him, and he did one-on-ones there for more than an hour.

It was remarkable to watch. Reggie knew the name of each writer and what paper he worked for. Big paper writers could ask anything. Writers from smaller, suburban papers were a different story?

"That's a stupid question," he said, although it hadn't been when a reporter with the Times, Post or Newsday had asked it. If that was a skilled performance, what followed was the stuff of legend.

The game began in the rain and eventually was shortened by bad weather. The Angels had to face one of the best left-handed pitchers in the game, Ron Guidry. Jackson, a left-handed hitter, batted seventh in the lineup – far from the heart-of-the-order spot he'd occupied throughout his career.

Late in the game, with the rain worsening, Reggie came up to face Guidry, and improbably, hit his first home run of the season. A sell-out crowd stood and cheered him, and as he rounded the bases, former Yankee teammates shouted out congratulations.

Then that crowd, which had loved Jackson throughout his New York career, began chanting.

"Steinbrenner sucks!"

It went on for minutes, in Steinbrenner's ballpark, as the fans insulted the team owner for letting Reggie go.

When the game was finally cancelled because of the rain, Reggie wasn't at his locker by the time the press was allowed in. On a hunch, I left, walked down the damp tunnel to the visiting dugout.

And there was Reggie, staring out at the field where he'd been a World Series hero, built up Hall of Fame credentials, and enjoyed each moment.

He glanced at me, almost vibrating with adrenaline.

"You have no idea what it's like to be me," Reggie said quietly. "Sometimes I can't believe what it's like. Tonight was … magical."

After hitting one home run in the first month of 1982, Reggie finished with 39 to lead the American League. He would play five more seasons, four of those in Anaheim, and finish his career with 563 home runs.

When he was elected to the Hall of Fame, I thought all the Reggies must have been delighted. I knew for a fact Reggie – any one of his personalities – could be … magical.

Bruce Kison: Nobody Wanted On His Hit Parade

A skinny right-hander whose fastball tailed back into right-handed hitters, Bruce Kison never hit more than 11 batters in any one big league season. It just seemed like he did.

Once, in a minor league game with future major league umpire Ken Kaiser behind the plate, Kison got to the sixth inning with a two-hitter – but he'd hit five home-team batters.

Kaiser went to the mound to chat.

"He told me, 'Son, I know you're not trying to hit anybody, but this crowd is getting restless. You hit anyone else, I'm going to run you,'" Kison said.

"I said, 'Thank you, sir.'"

Kaiser went back behind the plate. Kison returned to the mound.

"I hit the next guy in the neck," Kison said. "He ran me."

At 6-4, 178 pounds, Kison was fearless on a mound. He pitched sick, hurt, and at times when team doctors advised against it.

In 1982, Kison had back problems that caused his right leg to go almost numb.

The Angels were in a pennant race and Kison started a game for them in Milwaukee. As he delivered each pitch, his right leg would belatedly drag itself across the mound behind him. It was unnerving for hitters. He shouldn't have pitched, but he did, and he won.

No teammate ever doubted Kison's determination. And hitters never wondered what he'd do if they looked too comfortable at the plate.

Bobby Knoop: It Wasn't His Glove Or His Bat

In 1981, when the relationship between Angels manager Jim Fregosi and Rod Carew sailed well beyond testy, Carew told writers if he ran into the manager he might well flatten him.

Bobby Knoop, one of Fregosi's best friends and an Angels coach, listened and then approached Carew.

"Why don't you start with me?" Knoop asked.

Carew wanted no part of Knoop, who was then 53.

Knoop was a rawhide-tough man whose skills included gourmet cooking and the ability to finish the New York Times Sunday crossword – using a fountain pen – in under 20 minutes.

He was too old school to want anyone to know about those talents, and coached the way he had played. Knoop was a 'little ball' player for the expansion-team Angels. He was good with a glove, a bunt, a hit-and-run grounder or the hard slide at second that broke up the double play.

As a coach, he did his job without taking credit for it. If he had managerial ambitions, his sense of honor wouldn't allow him to campaign at the expense of the men he worked for.

Above all, Knoop was a realist.

On the team bus one day I asked him what had gotten him to the majors, his glove or his bat.

"Expansion," Knoop said.

Casey Kotchman: Not A Smiley Guy

When Casey Kotchman reported to spring training in 2010, I saw him talking to a friend, saw a great smile and snapped a photo.

Over the next eight months, I never saw that smile again.

Part of it was understandable. Kotchman wanted to bat third and, early on, did so. He struggled in April – the entire Seattle team did – and was dropped in the batting order.

The team continued to lose. Kotchman was at odds with manager Don Wakamatsu, believing he hadn't been given time to prove himself. He didn't like talking to the media.

That may not be strong enough.

Kotchman wouldn't talk to the media, and by June he would often walk away without a word when approached by reporters.

At season's end, I was handing out photo disks to all players. When I walked up to Kotchman at his locker he immediately threw a hand up to stop me.

"I don't have time to talk right now," he said.

"Casey, I'm trying to give you something," I said.

Kotchman shrugged. I left the disk. We never spoke again.

A year later, he was playing in Tampa Bay, I heard what a great guy he was. I suppose it could be true. When the Rays came through Seattle that year, he walked quickly into the training room when writers approached to say hello.

He still wasn't smiling.

Tony LaRussa: Willing To Share His Wisdom

Tony LaRussa was almost universally disliked by the beat writers who covered his managerial career in Chicago, Oakland and St. Louis – though none of them ever suggested he couldn't manage.

To those who followed him every day, LaRussa apparently was arrogant, overly-sensitive and condescending by turn.

Visiting writers? We loved him.

LaRussa was among the more fascinating – and successful – managers in major league history, a man who won a World Series managing in the American and National Leagues, a man who ranked third all-time in wins.

He was also a lawyer, an animal rights activist who founded his own rescue center, a vegetarian and a friend to Bruce Springsteen. Most important, he was always a good quote.

Over the years, I'd approached LaRussa and always found him accommodating. I'm sure he never recalled my name, but, we always exchanged pleasantries even when I didn't need an interview.

In the third month of his second year as a big league manager, Don Wakamatsu had gone from franchise hero in 2009 to a man whose job was in jeopardy not quite midway through 2010.

I liked Wakamatsu, respected him and was a little stunned at the lack of support he'd gotten from the team front office during a miserable start to his second season.

By the time the Mariners played an inter-league series in

St. Louis that June, Wakamatsu had taken the blame for the "mishandling" of Ken Griffey Jr., who had retired with a telephone call as he drove home.

Just as bad, when an unhappy and underachieving Chone Figgins initiated a dugout confrontation after being pulled from a game, general manager Jack Zduriencik responded with silence.

Nobody had Wak's back that summer, and I had already written that his job was in jeopardy.

In St. Louis the first day of the series, I was in Wak's office and somehow LaRussa's name came up.

"I know Bobby Cox and Sparky Anderson, managers I've admired and talked to over the years," Wakamatsu said. "I don't really know Tony, but he's been through it all. He's won 100 games in a season and lost 90 in a season.

"I'd love to talk to him about how he's dealt with that, just pick his brain on baseball."

I asked if he were serious or just paying LaRussa compliments. Wakamatsu said he was serious.

During Cardinals batting practice a bit later, I walked over to LaRussa and held up a finger.

"One minute?" I asked.

"Of course," he said.

"I have a young manager who'd love to spend a little time with you talking about baseball and life," I said. And then I started to tell him about Wakamatsu.

"I've watched him from a distance and I like the way he handles a game, I like the way he handles himself," LaRussa said. "My wife is out of town and this week after games I spend an hour reading, having a glass of wine and then heading home.

"If Don would like to join me, I'd be happy to have his company."

I thanked Tony and hustled over to Don's office and passed along the invitation. Wakamatsu's smile was the first genuine one I'd seen in a few weeks.

The next day I cornered Wakamatsu in his office alone. The smile was still there.

"We spent a couple of hours talking about everything – baseball and life," he said. "He told me the most important thing for any manager was the backing of his front office because without it, any time the team struggled you were going to be fired.

"He told me he'd done some of his best managing in some of his team's worst seasons, that sometimes getting through those years made him and his team better the next season."

Wakamatsu's spirits were clearly elevated. At 47, he was in his second year as a major league manager. LaRussa, 65, was managing in his 21st.

On the final day of the series, I found LaRussa in the Cardinals dugout and thanked him for his generosity.

"It was my pleasure," LaRussa said. "I enjoyed getting to know Don. He's been respected as a coach for a long time in this game, and he had a great first season in Seattle. I hope they're patient with him."

They weren't. On Aug. 6, about six weeks after Wakamatsu sat down with LaRussa, the Mariners fired him.

When I talked to Wakamatsu a few weeks later, the hurt in his voice was evident. He said he'd heard from a lot of baseball friends, sympathizing with him and wishing him well.

Wakamatsu said one that meant as much as any to him was a short note from St. Louis – Tony LaRussa's.

The next time I was in Oakland, near LaRussa's no-kill Animal Rescue Foundation in Walnut Creek, I stopped by and made a donation.

Fred Lynn: Does Playing Hurt, Hurt The Team?

Fred Lynn spent 17 graceful years in major league base-ball, and in most of them failed to reach the success of his first, when he was the American League's Rookie of the Year *and* its Most Valuable Player.

Quick with a smile and a quip, Lynn was a media favorite from his first days in Fenway Park to his final games with San Diego.

Always, he was compared to the Lynn of that first season. And frequently, he was criticized for what was perceived as a reluctance to play hurt.

The case could be made that Lynn's career was spotted with as many missed games as highlights. Only once in his career did he play as many as 150 games, and over his last 11 seasons he played as many as 140 only once.

At 6-1, 190 pounds, Lynn was fast and fearless in the '70s and '80s. Few All-Stars paid a higher price. There was no fence Lynn wouldn't challenge and few that didn't get the better of him.

In the mid-90s, I watched Ken Griffey Jr. outrun a ball in Tigers Stadium, fling himself into the fence in mad pursuit and make the catch – taking the cross bar of the wall in the ribcage.

He was sore for days, but ESPN replayed it for a week. Lynn had made almost the same impossible play more than a decade earlier – and lost weeks to the ensuing rib injury.

That was the cost of Lynn's style. If he played, he expected to catch anything any center fielder in the game could reach. When he was hurt, he thought playing weakened his team.

Not all of Lynn's managers and teammates agreed. Some questioned his pain threshold in clubhouses where playing in pain was more assumption than reality.

In Anaheim, players such as Don Baylor, Bobby Grich and Brian Downing played unless they were broken and by their standard Lynn fell short. On the other hand, Angels teammates such as Doug DeCinces, Dan Ford and Rod Carew sat with aches and strains.

So why was Lynn's reputation so tied to his missed games?

Much of it went back to that mythical first year in Boston, when he batted .331 with 47 doubles, 21 home runs and 105 RBI as a rookie savior for Boston

After 1975, it took him five years to match those numbers. By 1981, he was traded – another in a long series of heroes who had failed to lead Boston to a World Series.

Lynn was athletic, competitive and more than a little amused by his own image. Disappointments that haunted others didn't burden him. He wouldn't let them.

If he'd done his best – like when he batted over .600 for the losing team in the American League Championship Series in 1982 – Lynn wouldn't second guess himself.

More articulate than most teammates and better educated, Lynn was a man without airs. During the off-season he played pickup basketball with a group of friends, including one sportswriter.

One day he asked me to drive him to the gym. Afterward, he wanted to be dropped at a Porsche dealership.

There, I watched Fred Lynn write a check for a top-of-the-line Porsche. As I stood there thinking we lived in different worlds, Lynn glanced up at me, smiled and winked.

Lynn got it. He enjoyed life on and off the field, declined to take anything anyone said too seriously. He knew what he could do and when he could do it.

John Mabry: Keeping It In Perspective

John Mabry had the good fortune to play with Mark McGwire in St. Louis, although not everyone found that charming. On one of the few occasions McGwire did not start at first base in 1998, Mabry did.

"We were in Milwaukee and I'm in the on-deck circle and this guy in the first row looks at me and says, 'I didn't pay $80 to sit here and watch you hit!'" Mabry recalled. "So I started kidding him. I asked him if he'd buy me a beer if I hit a home run for him. He said he would."

And on the first pitch thrown to him, Mabry did just that.

Before his next at-bat, that fan had departed and Mabry thought no more about it. A few days later an usher delivered a six-pack of beer to the St. Louis clubhouse to Mabry – with a note signed by the fan.

"It read 'I congratulate you for talking the talk and walking the walk,'" Mabry said. "I kept that note."

Mabry was a player who worked hard to get to the big leagues, harder still to stay there. And when his role changed from starter to utility player to occasional pinch hitter, Mabry kept it all in perspective.

He started games in right field, left field, third base and first base, playing with and against the best players of his generation. He came to work early, left late, and never considered himself more than a few steps ahead of the guy who bought his way into the park.

"Would I rather start every day? Sure," he said. "But then

I remember I'm playing in the major leagues, and I think I could find a few million people who'd swap job complaints with me. There are worse places to watch a game than from the bench."

In a clubhouse where he was never a star, Mabry was a favorite. No one, especially himself, was immune from his irreverent teasing. It delighted him in Seattle when television crews continually confused him with teammate John Halama – and Mabry would do entire interviews without letting them know they had the wrong man.

One afternoon in Boston, Mabry grabbed the newspaper and walked out into still-empty Fenway Park and sat in the stands in his shorts and t-shirts.

I took a picture of him there, and he caught me and feigned indignation.

"You're going to make it look like I'm taking a dump in Fenway Park, aren't you?" Mabry asked, then paused.

"Send me a copy."

Josias Manzanillo: Line Drive Puts Him Down

Josias Manzanillo spent too many years in the minor leagues not to appreciate every moment he got in the majors, and his enthusiasm was more electric than his fastball.

Up and down as a reliever, Manzanillo was with Seattle in 1997 and started the season strong. He won over fans and teammates by sprinting off the mound at the end of any assignment.

What Manzanillo had never done in the big leagues was stay consistent – or wear a protective cup. In '97, the latter stopped the former.

On the mound of the Kingdome, the right-hander took a line drive up the middle in the worst conceivable spot and went down like anyone struck in the testicles would. Teammates surrounded him on the field, and one of them, Joey Cora, kept trying to encourage his pitcher.

"You've got to run off the field, like you always do," Cora said.

How Manzanillo managed to stand – let alone sprint – is inexplicable. The baseball had ruptured a testicle, and he'd need surgery before the night was over.

But stand he did. And sprint off the field he did – to a huge ovation.

Edgar Martinez: He Never Forgot Who He Was

The first time the Seattle Mariners offered him a contract, Edgar Martinez turned them down because he had everything he wanted – a factory job and a new Toyota.

"I was playing baseball three nights a week, making $30 a game," Martinez told me. "They offered me $2,000, and I didn't think it was worth it."

He was 20-years-old, living in Puerto Rico with the grandparents who'd raised him. Edgar's grasp of English was minimal, and he hadn't been in the United States since leaving New York after his first birthday.

"I told them I wanted a two-year contract, because I thought that might give me enough time to make an impression," he said.

They upped the offer: two years, $4,000.

That's how the Mariners landed a man who would be called the greatest right-handed hitter of his generation by his peers.

It was also the perfect introduction to Edgar Martinez.

As much as he loved baseball, there were practical aspects of his life that kept him grounded. It wasn't the money he pursued – he thought what he made in Puerto Rico was enough to live happily on.

I first interviewed him in the spring of 1989, and he was a reluctant rookie for the most charming of reasons.

"I don't like to talk about myself. I don't like to read about myself," he told me. "I do interviews because I think it's ...

polite."

He was 26-years-old at the time, just beginning a career that would see him play major league baseball through his 41st birthday. When he retired, it would be with two batting titles, seven All-Star selections and a .312 career average.

On teams where Ken Griffey Jr. and Randy Johnson were lightning rods, where Alex Rodriguez became a star, and Jay Buhner was the clown prince, Martinez was the heart of the Mariners.

"It took him six years in the minors to get here and he had to hit – what – .360 his last season just to get a chance?" manager Lou Piniella asked me. "What were they looking at?"

Bitterness could have accompanied his eventual ascension, but Edgar never showed it. A third baseman who hit for high average but little power early on, Martinez didn't get as many as 100 big league at bats until his eighth professional season. He lost years to the poor scouting, then more time to injury.

After winning an American League batting title in 1992, when he hit .343, Martinez came to spring training in '93 as a budding star. On the last day of camp, he tore a hamstring muscle and missed 120 games.

"It bothered me from March until December," he told me the next spring. "I wondered if I was done, if my leg would ever heal."

It did. Martinez batted .400 in the spring of 1994, and on opening day – his first at-bat – Cleveland's Dennis Martinez hit him with a pitch and broke his hand.

Edgar missed 73 games, and shouldn't have played in most of the 89 he did. He was 31-years-old and feeling like a one-season wonder.

"There were two directions he could have gone, and one of

them was home," Buhner said. "But 'Gar came back in '95 and look what happened."

Martinez showed up healthy, bigger and stronger. He won his second batting title, hitting .356 with an on-base percentage of .479. The Mariners made the post-season for the first time in their history, but then fell behind the New York Yankees in the best-of-five Division Series, 2-0.

Martinez led Seattle back to the most dramatic series win in franchise history. Faced with elimination, Edgar had seven RBI in Game 4, then drove in the tying and winning runs in the 11th inning of Game 5.

For the series, he batted .571.

"I've never seen anyone hit like that," Don Mattingly said afterward.

"The games mattered," Edgar told me years later. "For all of us, until that year, the games had never really mattered – we weren't in a pennant race.

"What we found out that year was when the games did matter, doing well was so much more fun. Winning was the difference."

I remember asking Edgar when he'd first fallen in love with baseball.

"My grandfather was a cab driver. He worked hard, and sometimes I would go with him," he said. "He had never played baseball, but I wanted to and he knew it."

The year he'd turned 6, Edgar got a uniform for Christmas – and 35 years later, he'd never forgotten it.

"White with stripes and my name on the back," he said. "My brother and I each had one, and we were the only kids in the area who did. Before I outgrew it, it was in tatters."

On Saturdays, when he played, his grandfather would come and sit on the bench with Edgar and his teammates.

"He didn't know the game well, but he liked being there

with me," Martinez said. "He wouldn't say much, but I liked having him there."

When he was 12, Edgar's parents remarried in New York, and his brother and sister went home to be with them. Edgar's choice? To stay with his grandparents in Puerto Rico.

With that $4,000 bonus he signed, Martinez bought them a home. For years afterward, at the end of each baseball season, he would return to Puerto Rico, to that house, and to his grandparents.

"They were there when I needed them, I had to be there for them," he said.

Most of his teammates never knew why Martinez went to Puerto Rico every winter. He wasn't the most talkative fellow in the clubhouse. I asked Norm Charlton once if Edgar ever said anything.

"He doesn't have to," Charlton said. "We were in the spring clubhouse and a bunch of the young guys – rookies – had a boom box on the floor playing really loud music.

"It was about 10 feet from Edgar's locker, and he kind of slowly stood up, walked over to that boom box and hit it with his bat – the thing blew into a hundred pieces.

"Then he went back to his stool and sat down. Message delivered."

Oh, and the next day, Charlton said, Martinez delivered a new boom box to the clubhouse.

Over the years in Seattle, Edgar became a fan favorite, showing up in one team commercial after another. There were Edgar Martinez Teddy Bear promotions, Edgar lunch pails, Edgar Rubber Ducky Nights.

And when he endorsed a local spa dealership, he was pictured sitting in a Jacuzzi relaxing – an ad that startled my wife.

"He doesn't have nipples," she said.

Sure enough, either the spa bubbles or the photographer had eliminated Edgar's nipples. I told him the story and he thought it was hilarious.

I had taken hundreds of photos of him by then, and in one he was making a funny face at me. I blew it up, told him he had the chance to set the record straight for my wife - did he or didn't he have nipples?

He carefully wrote on the photo:

"Marie, yes, I do – Edgar Martinez."

Tino Martinez: The Best Revenge

In spring training before the 1991 season, the News Tribune asked me to find a rookie willing to write – well, dictate – a weekly in-camp diary. I asked Tino Martinez.

I regretted that for years.

Tino was 23 that spring, coming off a marvelous season in Class AAA. He was, by any standard, the first baseman of the future for the Seattle Mariners.

And then general manager Woody Woodward, given an influx of cash by new owner Jeff Smulyan, did the unthinkable. He signed free agent first baseman Pete O'Brien to a multi-year deal – blocking Tino's path to the big leagues and breaking the heart of the franchise's first star, first baseman Alvin Davis.

Davis was made the designated hitter. O'Brien was the first baseman.

And Tino? He had no chance to make the team from Day 1, but he was clearly the best rookie in camp. So I asked, he accepted, and we tried to get through it.

Manager Jim Lefebvre, who would be fired that year, almost got me killed in the first installment of 'Who's On First?' In 24 games – 78 at-bats – the year before, Martinez had batted just .221,

"I thought he looked a little overmatched at times last year, like when he went through that 1-for-28 slump," Lefebvre said the first time I asked him about Martinez.

I thought it sounded a lot like a manager explaining why a

rookie wasn't going to make the team – weeks before a decision was necessary. But he said it, I wrote it.

Mid-week, a teammate found a copy of the article, high-lighted Lefebvre's quote, and gave it to Tino.

"It sounded to me like Jim was looking for an easy way to send me down if he has to," Tino said in our next installment. "Using that slump isn't fair. That was last year, and to use it as an excuse to send me down again this year wouldn't be fair."

That quote, in turn, irritated Lefebvre, and it became obvious to me I'd put Tino on the spot with this diary business.

Over the course of the next few weeks, Martinez rarely started a game, and when he did play, it was often against left-handed pitchers he'd never seen – the worst-case scenario for a left-handed rookie hitter.

The last 'diary' was painful, but the kid was honest and held up his end.

"I've got no chance of making the team and I haven't for a couple of weeks," he said. "I'm not asking for a trade, but a trade would be fine with me.

"I kept trying to tell myself if I played well it would matter, but I didn't believe it."

To his credit, Tino went back to Class AAA and had another marvelous year. By '92, Lefebvre was gone, and Martinez got his chance. Over the next four years, he improved to the point where – in 1995 – he hit 31 home runs and had 111 RBI.

With both Edgar Martinez and Tino Martinez playing key roles for the Mariners in those years, I came up with a short-hand way of referring to them in stories – The Edgar and The Tino.

After the '95 season, the Mariners decided they couldn't afford what Martinez was going to command in the years ahead, so they traded him to the New York Yankees.

How'd that work out?

Tino Martinez was part of a Yankees run that saw the team win the World Series four years in a row, and he averaged 27 home runs and 106 RBI the next seven seasons.

Against all odds, and despite that silly rookie diary, Tino was always open and friendly with me. In New York, he became a star and had to live with the demands of stardom in The Big Apple.

His life had changed, and he tried to be professional without losing his privacy.

"I talk to the media almost every day, before and after games," he told me. "Then I leave it here. I don't want TV crews in my home. I don't want to spend off days with writers I don't know, answering the same questions I answered at the ballpark.

"Everyone wants something unique, but I can't help them. I'm doing the same things this year I've done every other year – I'm just having a better season."

I asked how long it had taken him to forgive me getting him into that camp diary in '92.

"You didn't sign Pete O'Brien and you weren't Jim Lefebvre," he said.

If the best revenge is living well, Tino got his. Before he retired, he'd played in 99 playoff games while the Mariners as a franchise had appeared in 33.

Seattle had never been to the World Series. Tino was in five of them, and won four rings.

Don Mattingly: Last Game Was His Best

Don Mattingly was an agile, graceful first baseman with the New York Yankees en route to a Hall of Fame career when back problems reduced him to mortality.

By his 14th season, in 1995, Mattingly knew retirement was imminent, and few knew the constant pain with which he played his final seasons.

Throughout his tenure in New York, his team had never been to the playoffs. Then, in his last season – '95 - they got the American League Division Series against a franchise that had never been in the post-season, the Seattle Mariners.

The best of five series went to a fifth game, then into extra innings. In the 11th inning, New York scored to take the lead. Impossibly, in the bottom of the 11th, Seattle scored twice to win.

Mattingly, 34, had played his final game. In that five-game series, he batted .414 with a home run and six RBI. He drove in two runs in Game 5.

In the Mariners clubhouse, champagne was being sprayed on everyone and I made my way toward Edgar Martinez, whose double had won the game.

Soaked in champagne, Edgar began talking and then stopped. Don Mattingly stood in the Seattle clubhouse, watching the celebration. Martinez went to him and the two embraced. Manager Lou Piniella came out of his office and joined them.

"I wanted to say congratulations," Mattingly said. "That

was the best game I ever played in."

Piniella teared up. So did Mattingly and Martinez and a parade of Mariners – Jay Buhner, Ken Griffey Jr., Mike Blowers – who realized Mattingly was retiring and wanted to say goodbye.

Afterward, Mattingly walked back to the Yankee clubhouse and took off his uniform for the last time as a player.

"What that says about Don Mattingly is all you need to know about a man," Piniella said.

Gene Mauch: He Managed The Way He Played

Gene Mauch played baseball in an era when if a base runner slid into second base head first, middle infielders made a point of stomping his hands with their spikes. Mauch was one of those infielders.

He managed the same way. On the top step of the dugout nearest home plate, Mauch was a brilliant needler – capable of getting under the skin of nearly any opposing player. It wasn't a character flaw, it was as orchestrated as every aspect of Mauch's actions as a manager.

Mostly, he managed poor teams – expansion clubs and second-division squads. The poorer his talent, the tougher his heckling became. Mauch wanted to be a distraction to the other team. It might just give his team an edge.

Opposing players often detested him. If you were on his team, Mauch would fight for you – literally. Once in Montreal, Mauch's shortstop, Tim Foli was beaned by Steve Carlton. Foli was down, so Mauch charged the mound in his stead.

"He pounded my head like a tom-tom," Mauch recalled of Carlton. "I think he was glad I came."

No one knew the rules of the game better. Mauch could glance at a box score and break down the game for both teams, tell you why each pinch-hitter came into the game an how the opposing manager responded.

His managerial career spanned 26 years and accounted for 1,902 major league wins. For most, he was remembered as the best manager who never won it all, for Philadelphia's late collapse in '64, for the Angels post-season losses in '82 and '86.

Baseball was Mauch's life. In 1982, I asked him when was the last time that he'd gone to the movies.

"Not since that little girl with the curly hair stopped making them," he said.

Translation: Not since Shirley Temple's childhood films.

Mauch wasn't one-dimensional. He was intensely competitive, in golf and cards as much as in baseball. Intensely private, he considered the media a necessary evil but wouldn't stand still for long interviews.

"I won't lie on anybody's couch," he said. "Analyze someone else."

One criticism of Mauch was that he thought too much, that he wanted to show the world he could win by outsmarting it.

And when he lost, as all managers do, Mauch explained why he'd done what he'd done. If you didn't understand it then, he would shake his head and shrug.

The last time I saw him, Mauch was alone in the Kansas City Royals dugout during a rain delay – testing a batting stance, rocking slowly to get his balance. I approached and couldn't resist. What was he doing?

"Trying to remember how I used to hit," Mauch said.

"You never forgot anything in your life," I said.

And for one of the few times in the years we knew one another, Mauch looked at me and smiled.

"You're right," he said. And winked.

Willie Mays: A Talk in the Park

In the spring of 1988, a few dozen young San Francisco Giants minor league players stood on the infield getting personal tips on base-running from a man who had their complete attention.

Willie Mays.

He explained the lost art of the hook slide, the 'fade away' slide. Looking at a few blank faces, he shrugged.

"Ok, then just watch me," he said.

Willie Howard Mays got a running start and then demonstrated the hook slide. Then a fade-away slide. About the sixth time Mays slid, he tore his uniform pants at the knee, opening a small cut on his knee.

Mays was 57-years-old. And beaming.

I had an interview scheduled with Mays that day, and when the workout was over, he walked over to me – limping slightly – his left knee a bit bloodied and stiff.

We walked over to a picnic bench. He hopped up on the table.

Mays talked about the pain of a brief ban from baseball when he and Mickey Mantle had taken jobs with a casino to play golf with high rollers.

He talked about a lifelong love for the game, and about what it was like to feel forgotten by a generation of players who thought the 30-30 club - 30 stolen bases, 30 home runs—was the stuff of automatic enshrinement.

"I did that twice, and we didn't run then like they run

now," Mays said. "You ran to change a game. When it didn't matter, you didn't run. I could always steal a base."

Mays stole 338 of them, not an overwhelming total – but in 1970 he stole 23 bases in 26 attempts. That season he turned 39.

Often portrayed as bitter, Mays certainly wasn't that day. As we talked about baseball, two things happened. He became more animated – and fans walking past us recognized him.

And they stayed to listen.

Eventually, there were more than 25 of them, sitting around the picnic bench. Not once did anyone interrupt the interview. People sat on the grass and simply listened to a legend tell stories.

Willie Mays talked about base-running and home runs, playing center field in the Polo Grounds and then in the winds that were so much a part of Candlestick Park.

He talked about Leo Durocher and Willie McCovey, Sandy Koufax and a few dozen other favorites.

"Bob Gibson was a friend unless he was starting the next day," Mays said. "Then he'd put one in your ear hole. I was never afraid to face him until we had dinner together one night and he put on glasses to read the menu.

"I said, 'Bob, you don't wear glasses.' And he said, 'I can't see a thing without them.' Next day in the batters box, I looked out at him on the mound and realized he wasn't wearing glasses."

Our audience laughed. When the interview ended, those who'd been listening stood up and began clapping. It was the only interview I ever conducted that got a standing ovation.

That's what Willie Mays means to those who love baseball.

Jack McKeon: Old Man In Young Man's Game

The year Jack McKeon managed the Florida Marlins to a World Series championship, he won the loyalty of a team that at one point had been 10 games below .500.

He just couldn't keep their names straight.

"That whole season, he called me 'Luis,'" outfielder Juan Pierre said. "And every time he talked about Luis Castillo, he'd call him 'Juan.'"

McKeon was 72 that season and, eight years later, came out of the Marlins front office in mid-season to manage again at age 80–the second oldest manager in big league history.

His first game back, he benched the team star, Hanley Ramirez, for not hustling. When he learned players were often in the clubhouse instead of on the bench during games, McKeon took care of that without saying a word.

He had the doors to the clubhouse locked during games.

A terrible switch-hitting catcher during a lengthy minor league career, McKeon later insisted he hit three ways - "left-handed, right-handed and seldom."

"I hit .300 one season," he deadpanned. "I hit .150 left-handed and .150 right-handed."

When McKeon took the Marlins job in 2011, it was 38 years after he'd first managed a big league team. The game had changed, the players had changed.

McKeon had not.

Before games, he had once run laps around the field. At 80, after knee and hip surgeries, he walked. In '73 and '11, he allowed himself one huge cigar before a game and another after.

Before games, he liked to sit in the stands near the dugout, watching his players, smoking a cigar and holding court with all comers.

He never missed a thing. One day in Seattle a few of us were talking to him in the stands when one of his infielders, who'd been running on his own, started off the field.

"You work that hard, you ought to have a little more company," McKeon said.

The next afternoon, the player came out for early work again – and three other Marlins were with him.

At 80, McKeon looked 60, and though he still forgot first names he had no trouble getting his messages across. The secret to longevity?

"Baseball and a lot of salads," he said.

McKeon always managed with the thought that it was an honor to wear a major league uniform, and that he – and his players – had to conduct themselves in a way that paid respect to those who'd come before them.

Upon his return to the game at 80, he was the punch line of every joke media types could come up with. One asked if he'd need a seventh inning nap. Another wondered if McKeon would take the lineup to home plate each night in a motorized cart.

A week into his 2011 tenure, he took post-game questions for 20 minutes then waved writers off.

"C'mon, guys," he said. "Betty White is waiting up for me.

Kevin Mitchell: Hard To Stay Out Of Trouble

Sportswriters didn't follow Kevin Mitchell around, though they should have. Everywhere the man went, stories broke out.

The Most Valuable Player in the National League in 1989, Mitchell was a kid who'd grown up in a Southern California neighborhood with plenty of friends who were members of street gangs.

After he made the big leagues, Mitchell once spent $19,000 on stereo equipment for his car. Never one to turn his back on old friends, he loaned that car to a childhood buddy – who was arrested for murder while driving it.

A hitter with extraordinary power, Mitchell's biggest problem was staying in shape and healthy.

The year he spent with the Seattle Mariners, he would eat heartily late in the afternoon, them shove a big finger down his throat and vomit.

"Lightening up," he called it when he demonstrated for those of us willing to watch.

Once, he threw up so violently he strained an oblique muscle and missed a half-dozen games.

In San Francisco, he reported late to spring training one year, saying he had needed emergency dental surgery. Why? Mitchell said he had put a frozen donut in his microwave, overheated it – and blown out several fillings when he bit into boiling chocolate.

His most famous on-field play can still be viewed on

YouTube and bloopers videos shown at ballparks, though it was made in 1989.

An outfielder, Mitchell was in St. Louis' Busch Stadium, chasing a ball hit by Ozzie Smith toward the left field corner. Mitchell got to the ball, but inexplicably reached out - on the dead run - and caught it with his bare hand.

Unable to stop, Mitchell banged into an unlatched door that led under the stands - and simply disappeared.

When he emerged, he was beaming, a gold front tooth shining.

Mitchell was capable of bad temper and had occasional run-ins with the law, during and after a long major league career.

In 2000, he was the player-manager in the Independent Leagues for the Sonoma Crushers, making $2,200 a month. When a pitcher – former Mariners Jim Converse – threw a pitch behind him, Mitchell charged the mound.

That wasn't good, but what followed was worse. Mitchell disliked what a guy in the stands near the dugout yelled at him, so he punched him, too.

It was the owner of the home team Solano Steelheads.

Robert Fletcher, the owner of Mitchell's team, was quick to his defense.

"Kevin thought the guy was a fan," Fletcher insisted.

In 2011, Mitchell took up a gentleman's game, golf, and of course writers should have followed him around.

On the 13th hole of a lovely San Diego course, Mitchell and one of his playing partners got into a debate about a mutual golf instructor. Mitchell liked him, his partner did not.

So Mitchell slugged him

In court, Mitchell was given three-year's probation and ordered to undergo 120 hours of anger management.

Paul Molitor: He Did What He Had To Do

When I first met Paul Molitor, he was nearly as full of himself as I was – a predicament that life slowly resolved in us both.

By the time we worked in the same place – when he became the Seattle Mariners' hitting coach in 2004 – he'd been elected to the Hall of Fame, and I was a writer enjoying my job.

His path had been far more difficult.

Early on in a career that began in 1978, he was fast and loose and played hard on and off the field. There was a cocaine problem he corrected, then a series of injuries that cost him more than 600 games.

"Most guys couldn't have gone through what he went through," Milwaukee general manager Sal Bando said. "Most guys wouldn't have come back from half of it."

That was 1992. Molitor played six more seasons.

The injuries were debilitating. A torn elbow ligament, broken wrist, torn hamstrings, a broken thumb, a torn muscle in his rib cage, torn ligaments in his left ankle ...

"My career could have ended anywhere in those first 15 years," Molitor said. "For every injury, I've faced the challenge of coming back – and I've done it.

"Maybe because of all the time away with injuries, I appreciate the game more."

He came out of St. Paul as a pull hitter and started making adjustments in his first minor league season. Over the years, he hit to all fields.

Never considered a power hitter, Molitor hit 234 home runs, another 605 doubles and collected 3,319 hits.

As amazing as any of his numbers was this: After age 32, he collected more than a thousand hits – and did it faster than his first or second thousand, when he was far younger.

After his 32nd birthday, Molitor played nine more years. His batting average went ... up.

"Whether it was batting practice or a game, I never went to the plate just to swing," he said. "You teach yourself reaction – fastball, you do this, breaking pitch, you do that.

"But you've got to be thinking about it, you've got to be aware of so many things – the pitcher, the situation, the count, how that team has pitched you before ..."

Molitor had the reticent nature of a Lutheran, a man who would smile a greeting to you without saying a word. Engage him, he could be candid, but he was always cautious.

We talked about his childhood over the years, and he told me when he played baseball his mother never missed a game.

"It made her nervous, though, and she was always afraid I'd be watching her worry," Molitor said. "I'd have to try and find which tree she was hiding behind."

And the drug problem that cost him his reputation in the early '80s?

"I played in a time that mirrored society, and that was good and bad," Molitor said. "Players drank in the '60s. Players had other temptations in the '70s and '80s.

"How did I survive? I minimized that chapter in my life."

Molitor slowly changed the way fans saw him with a what-ever-it-takes attitude that, with the Milwaukee Brewers, saw him play every position but pitcher, catcher and left field.

"It wasn't that he couldn't play any one position well, it

was that he played them all well," teammate Robin Yount said.

And Molitor kept hitting, wherever he was.

With Toronto in 1993, Molitor was 37-years-old. He batted .332 in the regular season, then .500 in the World Series as the Blue Jays won a championship.

A free agent after the 1995 season, Molitor was 40 – and seven teams came after him. He signed, for considerably less than his best offer, with the Minnesota Twins.

Molitor wanted to go home, play in front of family and friends.

In his one year as a coach with the Mariners, Molitor was at times frustrated by hitters who were unwilling to change their approach or philosophy at the plate.

Hitters such as Bret Boone, Ichiro Suzuki, Miguel Olivo and John Olerud did it their way. Late in the season, Molitor took a few days off. He had baseball business to attend to.

The man hitters wouldn't always listen to flew to New York for his induction into the Hall of Fame.

Mike Morse: Clueless In Seattle

Mike Morse was a big, loopy kid who loved baseball and didn't quite grasp all the subtleties of a player's relationship with management.

The spring he turned 23, he wandered in to the Seattle Mariners clubhouse, a 6-foot-5 rookie without a single day in the big leagues, and met his new manager, the old-school Mike Hargrove.

"Hey, big dog," Morse said. "How's it hanging?"

Hargrove burst out laughing and left the development of Morse's sense of etiquette to the veteran players. It was obvious to everyone, including Hargrove, that Morse was not a smartass.

He was just clueless.

Large, strong and quick, Morse came to Seattle as a minor league shortstop from the Chicago White Sox, where – in 2004 – he was suspended for using steroids.

My first one-on-one interview with Morse, I asked about what had happened two years earlier, fully expecting the normal excuses. It had been a tainted power shake, his urine test must have been compromised, someone gave him something to try ...

"In November 2003, when I was 21-years-old, I took steroids," Morse said. "I'd torn a thigh muscle and it wouldn't heal and I was scared my career was over.

"I watched guys I'd played with moving up in the system and I couldn't, so I got desperate. I injected steroids to see if they would help me heal."

They did, but a drug test the next spring busted him.

"I didn't lie about it, I told the truth," Morse said. "I made a terrible mistake, and I made a promise to myself, my family, and this game never to make another like it."

We were still learning about steroids that year, wouldn't know the extent of usage for years to come. But no one who'd been caught taking them had ever admitted doing so.

Morse did.

Given a fresh start with a new team, he came to camp and worked hard, playing shortstop, first base, third base and, occasionally, the outfield. He wasn't particularly good at any of them.

But he could hit.

Brought up from AAA in 2005, he was batting .283 when major league baseball suspended him for steroid use. The day before it was announced, Morse called me aside.

"I went through a hearing and I'm going to be suspended again," he said. "But it's for the same stuff I took in '03. There's only trace evidence in my blood system, and even the panel agreed it was consistent with what would still be there from '03.

"I kept my promise. I never took anything again. But I'm going to be suspended."

Morse was suspended that year, and injuries marred his next two seasons.

In 2008, a new manager, John McLaren, was determined to get Morse's bat into his lineup and tried him in the outfield – the kid had batted .492 in spring training.

Pursuing a fly ball that April, Morse dove and ruined his left shoulder. Major reconstruction was required and he missed the year.

In 2009, there was a new manager – Morse's third in

Seattle – who didn't think much of his now 27-year-old prospect. Seattle traded Morse to the Washington Nationals for minor league outfielder Ryan Langerhans.

With the Nationals, Morse batted .285 platooning in 2010. It looked like, at last, he'd at least found a bench job. We e-mailed back and forth and he was excited going into the 2011 season, said he might finally win a starting spot in the lineup.

He insisted he'd stayed clean, that his vice now was working out – and that 6-foot-5 frame had filled out. His nickname in Washington: The Beast.

Morse won the job and appeared in a career-high number of games. He batted .300, hit 27 home runs, and drove in nearly 100.

Morse had become a big dog.

Jamie Moyer: Never Say It's Over, Until It's Over

He worked so hard and failed so miserably that, before his 34th birthday, Jamie Moyer had been released by five major league teams and traded by two more.

A few weeks after he was acquired by Seattle, I asked him how he'd maintained any degree of confidence.

"I'm sure at some point, I took offense to someone's opinion of me, but they were entitled to it," he said. "They still are. Right or wrong, they made decisions based on their opinions.

"Enough people have said I'm done over the years, and I keep proving them wrong. Eventually, they're going to be right."

Moyer turned 49 in the winter of 2011 when I last talked to him. He'd had a major elbow reconstruction in 2010 and at age 47, was finally considered finished.

Was he?

"Not yet," Moyer said.

Hall of Fame general manager Pat Gillick, now a special advisor with the Philadelphia Phillies, saw Moyer throw last winter. I asked what he'd seen in the veteran left-hander.

"I'll be frank – he looked the same as he always did," Gillick said. "He may be in better shape than he was in 2008, when he won 16 games for us."

Moyer is something of a freak in the buttoned down world of baseball opinion. He never threw hard and his 84-86 mph fastball was well below league average.

Working with that fastball, a slow curve and a slower than that changeup – clocked anywhere from 75 mph to 66 mph – Moyer managed to stay in the game.

By 33, however, he'd pitched with the Cubs, Rangers, Cardinals, Tigers, Orioles and Red Sox.

He'd won 79 games in his career, lost 80.

When he arrived in Seattle, manager Lou Piniella told him something no other manager ever had.

"I told him he was going to get the ball every fifth day, no matter what," Piniella said. "I like what Moyer can do."

Like what, I asked.

"Outside of a dominant fastball, the best pitch in baseball is a good changeup.

"When I played, Geoff Zahn had a great changeup – it was his best pitch. If I knew he was going to start one game in a series against us, I'd be thinking about him for days. Instead of making me more patient, it made me more antsy.

"He'd throw that slow change up there and I'd scream at him, and he'd throw it slower and I'd miss that, too," Piniella said. "A guy with a great changeup he can locate, he can win."

Moyer won – 17 games in his first full season as a Mariner, then 20 games in his sixth year, a club-record 21 in his eighth – the year he turned 40.

It wasn't by accident.

Moyer studied hitters and kept a book on each of them, jotting down what they liked in certain counts, how they'd hit this pitch or that, how he'd gotten them in a key situation.

Just playing catch, he'd work on location.

"If you're throwing, why not try to hit your partner's left hip, then his right? It's what you do on a mound, pitching inside, then out," Moyer said.

Every starting pitcher I'd ever known didn't want to talk to anyone the day he pitched. Moyer was the exception, and it could be unnerving.

Watching batting practice, I'd look over my shoulder and Moyer would be there watching the opposing team hit. Inevitably, he'd start a conversation and we'd be chatting and then I'd realize he was pitching in about 90 minutes.

Still, when he talked, he was fascinating.

"Hitting a changeup is all reaction. If I make it look like a fastball, the hitter is trained to react – 'fastball!'" he said. "No matter what else you throw, hitters are trained to look fastball first.

"If a hitter doesn't, he'll look foolish on a fastball. Even an 84 mph fastball. And hitters hate looking foolish."

Moyer smiled.

"You never see clinics on 'how to hit the changeup.' Hitters can be patient, selective, and they can give me trouble," he said. "But those kind of hitters give everyone trouble.

"Now, if a hitter goes to the plate against me trying to kill what I throw ... I gotcha."

The year Moyer turned 43, the Mariners traded him to Philadelphia, convinced he was finally nearing the end of a wonderful career. In the next four-plus seasons, Moyer won 56 games.

And, in 2008, a World Series title.

"You look at his numbers from the time he was traded to Seattle in '96, I doubt there are four or five pitchers in the game who are more games above .500 since then than Jamie," Gillick said.

"He's won – what – 267 games in his career?"

Gillick laughed.

"I don't think he's done. In fact, I made a call for him to an

American League general manager, told him I'd seen Jamie throw and he ought to take a look at him," Gillick said.

Moyer, as always, was succinct.

"I love the competition at baseball's highest level and I can still do that," he said. "Why would I stop? Some day it won't be my choice, for now it is. My choice is to pitch."

Tony Muser: A Fire Ball Couldn't Stop Him

All his life, Tony Muser thought the best place in the world to be was a major league clubhouse. Then one tried to kill him.

A lifetime spent in baseball as a player, minor league manager and big league coach nearly ended in the Milwaukee Brewers spring locker room. Dressing for the day's work, Muser was alone in the coaches' room on Feb. 27, 1986 when a gas line in the ceiling exploded – and a fire ball literally burned the uniform off his back, leaving 48 percent of his body burned.

Muser was so bloated by evening that his wife, flown in from California, fainted when she saw him. He was in critical condition for days. Months of surgery and painful rehabilitation followed.

Muser returned to baseball a year later on the condition that he wear long sleeves to protect skin grafts.

In the summer of 1997, he was named manager of the Kansas City Royals after having interviewed for 11 other managerial openings. Few men ever had tougher roads to that job.

Muser was a tough task master—especially by big league standards. After one rain-shortened loss, he had his team running wind sprints at Kauffman Stadium.

He wanted to instill the toughness that came naturally to him. The job didn't last. Muser did.

Jeff Nelson: Surrounded By Girls

At 6-foot-8, 235 pounds, Jeff Nelson was a presence on the mound, and threw a stand-there-at-your-own-peril slider to right-handed hitters that made him part of the New York Yankees four World Series victories in the late '90s.

Nelson could also change a Barbie doll's clothes while lying on his back in bed, half asleep.

In an era when most players let their hair grow longer, Nelson was the throw-back, sporting a flat top for most of his 15 seasons in the big leagues.

At home, he never lost touch with his softer side. He never had the chance.

"I'm way outnumbered at home," Nelson said. "There's my wife, our four girls - even our dog Sierra is female. Once I leave the ball park at night, my life is painting toe nails and braiding hair.

"I can't imagine life without them. I don't know how single guys do it. What's to stop them from thinking about the game 24/7?"

Drafted by the Los Angeles Dodgers the year he turned 18, Jeff and then-fiance Collette were still babies in their own right when they were married on the mound of a minor league ballpark when Nelson was 20.

Their families worried it wouldn't last.

During minor league stops in San Bernardino and Williamsport, Jacksonville and Calgary, the two were often apart for months. Collette stayed in school and became a nurse.

Nelson wound up with the Seattle Mariners, emerging as one of the premiere bullpen setup men in the game.

And the girls just kept on coming.

Chandler, Gabrielle, Emily and Alexandra.

Throughout the '95 season, when the Mariners made a push for their first post-season berth, players had taken note of Collette's growing belly and used it to their advantage.

"(Ken Griffey) Junior started rubbing her belly—calling her 'Budha Belly' before every game for luck," Nelson said. "It was funny, but it got to the point where everybody had to rub her belly before games."

The Mariners beat the Angels in a one-game playoff to win the American League West that year and, yes, Seattle players rubbed Collette's stomach before that game.

After beating New York in the American League Division Series, the Mariners ran out of luck and lost to Cleveland in the AL Championship Series – their good-luck charm delivered Chandler Grace.

Traded to New York after that '95 season, Nelson won four World Series rings, one for each of the girls. When he re-turned to the Mariners in 2001, he came back as a well-trained father.

"Collette is the disciplinarian, she handles all the hard stuff," Nelson said.

"I make them cereal in the morning when I'm home, and we have tea parties with the dog and the dolls.

"The girls would jump into bed with me some mornings and want their Barbies changed."

As they grew up, there were soccer games and swim meets, basketball games and plays to attend.

By 2006, arm problems hampered Nelson's ability to pitch. He moved into broadcasting, learning that craft at a small station, and then was hired in New York.

Collette and the kids stayed in Seattle. During Nelson's baseball season, he would spend five days a week in New York, and then fly home each weekend.

He loved baseball too much to walk away. And loved his girls too much to be gone full time.

John Olerud: A Man Of Few Words

Once he joined the Seattle Mariners in 2000, I had to trick John Olerud into talking every time I had to do a story on him.

I had interviewed Olerud a few times during his first 11 major league seasons. There were plenty of starting points. He'd never played minor league baseball, gone straight from college to the majors.

Olerud won a batting title the year he turned 24 – and a second World Series ring. He married the woman he had a high school crush on, though he'd been too shy to ask her out until college.

His conversational skills were the stuff of legend.

"I had the locker next to his last spring, and 'Hello' was a long conversation," teammate Norm Charlton said.

"I was his bridge partner in Toronto and I'd talk to him every day," Joe Carter told me. "He still hasn't started a conversation with me."

So interviewing Olerud meant you needed to find a topic that engaged him, brought some kind of response.

Always, he'd try to work with you.

"I'm just an average guy. I'm quiet. I like movies and golf and watching television," he told me earnestly. "I love my wife, my family and what I do for a living. People keep asking me what I'm really like – that's it."

One day, I asked him what the last spontaneous thing he'd

done was. Olerud thought for perhaps a full minute.

"I can't think of anything right now," he said.

Interviewing John was like a game where we were on the same side and trying to help one another. Sometimes, I had to warm him up.

Olerud had a reputation as a man who could and did eat anything, at any time of day or night, and not worry about his weight.

"Some crazy metabolism," he admitted.

Knowing his love of food, I asked him to name what snacks he could get in various big league clubhouses, and started dropping teams on him. He had an answer for each.

Tampa Bay? A Cuban sandwich.

Cleveland? Finger foods, cookies and banana bread.

Kansas City? A Slurpee machine.

Anaheim? Chili with cheese and onions.

By his third spring with the Mariners, finding the starting point had become a challenge. So I asked Olerud, a career .295 hitter, about a teammate who'd won two batting titles, Edgar Martinez.

He broke down Edgar's swing, his approach, talked about the way Martinez worked a pitcher, wasn't afraid to bat with two strikes. When he finished, we were both a bit surprised.

"Pretty good, huh?" Olerud asked.

For all that, Olerud emerged as a complete person with real life challenges and heartbreaks, not from any single interview but from years of talking to him three or four times a week.

As I saw it, part of my job was building relationships with the men in the game. And that meant talking to them not just when I needed a quote, but almost daily – mining for nuggets that might help later and also might let us know one another better.

Olerud was a technology nut, forever buying a watch that did five things or a cell phone with the ability to find any Starbucks in any city in America.

Late at night, when some teammates might be out carousing, Olerud liked nothing better than milk and a cookie.

Yet there was so much more.

In January of 1989, at age 20, Olerud had been the '88 NCAA Player of the Year when he collapsed after a workout. Taken to a local hospital in Spokane, Wash., he got a call from his father, John Olerud, Sr., who was a Seattle doctor.

He wanted his son to be moved to Seattle for further tests. Olerud went, and the tests found an aneurysm in his brain.

"I was stunned," Olerud said of the diagnosis. "I was an athlete, I planned on being around another 50 or 60 years."

Six hours of delicate surgery repaired the aneurysm but left his head vulnerable to any impact. For the rest of his baseball career, Olerud wore a protective batting helmet – at the plate and in the field.

"After the aneurysm, I was going to make major changes in my life," Olerud told me. "I was going to be less introverted."

Did he change?

"No, not at all," he said, and laughed.

John and Kelly Olerud had a two-year-old son, Garrett, when their second child was born in 2000. It would change their lives forever, although Olerud had to be pushed to talk about it.

"When Jordan was born, she had some deletion in one chromosome and a little extra in a second one," he said. "The doctors ran her through a national data base, looking for similar cases.

"There weren't any. She's absolutely unique."

Jordan spent months in the hospital before coming home, had trouble ingesting food, trouble with her eyesight, her ability to recognize anyone. She needed constant care.

The Oleruds visited specialists across the country and found no one had a solution.

At the annual Mariners 'Fathers and Family' game at Safeco Field, Olerud brought Garrett, who romped with his peers, and Jordan, who watched and wandered the field with Kelley or John always nearby.

I asked John how he dealt with the daily challenges of a child like Jordan. When he answered, it was the longest response I'd ever heard him give.

"I remember holding her in the hospital when they tried to give her an IV once. They tried one arm, couldn't get it, then tried the other. Then they started with her feet," he said.

"Jordan is in my arms, looking at me like, 'Why are you letting them do this to me?' I wanted to tell her but I knew she wouldn't understand. She just had to trust me."

Olerud looked out on the field where his family was enjoying themselves, then continued.

"It's the same situation we're in with God," he said. "We have to trust what we don't understand. Even if He explained it, we might not understand.

"Our plan was to have healthy kids. God planned something else."

Jim Palmer: Baseball Legend With A Gift for Gab

Almost every encounter with Jim Palmer over the past 25 years has quickly turned to the same comment.

"I may not know much about pitching, but I did throw thirty-nine hundred and forty-eight innings and win 268 games," Palmer will say.

And he did.

At 6-foot-3 and 190 pounds, he was lean, strong and durable, and his Hall of Fame career spanned 20 years, during which his high leg kick was as well-known as his endless arguments with Baltimore manager Earl Weaver.

As a player, Palmer was certain he knew more about the game than Weaver. Once Palmer retired and was elected to the Baseball Hall of Fame, he seemed willing to accept he knew more about the game than anyone alive.

On the mound, he won three Cy Young Awards, three World Series championships, was named to six All-Star teams and won four Gold Glove Awards for fielding – all for one team, the Baltimore Orioles.

Palmer could pitch.

He could also talk, which drove Weaver crazy and would later serve Palmer in television commercials and a broad-casting career. In the '70s his male-model good looks made him a natural spokesman for Jockey's men's underwear ad campaigns.

Talking to Palmer often was more a matter of letting

Palmer talk. He didn't need questions, and over the years I would watch one young writer after another wade in, be buried alive with words and attempt to extricate themselves from what could become an eternal interview.

In fairness, Palmer had much worth talking about.

In truth, he would talk about it to anyone.

"I'd like to think someone who struck out 2,212 batters could help a young pitcher," Palmer told me once. "I'd like to think if I'd had the chance to listen to a pitcher who pitched in 575 games and won a World Series in three different decades, I'd have done so."

You might think so, but you'd be wrong.

Baltimore pitchers grew so weary of constantly hearing Palmer talk some of them chose to hide from him, like veteran Jamie Moyer.

"I'd go into the training room and sit there, because he wasn't allowed in," Moyer said. "Jim knows the game, but it just gets old at times."

Palmer never limited himself to Orioles pitchers. Each team the Orioles played was fair game, too. Young pitchers, especially, were good targets – those who knew Palmer as a Hall of Fame pitcher were delighted he would speak to them.

In 2011, the Mariners had a rookie pitcher named Tom Wilhelmsen and, when he walked into the visiting dugout at Camden Yards, he was taking in the field when Palmer meandered over.

I was leaning on the railing next to Wilhelmsen, and the 65-year-old Palmer extended his hand, shook with the rookie, nodded to me and then said something very kind.

"Tom, I've read good things about you," Palmer said.

Wilhelmsen might never have been happier.

"I understand you're a fastball-slider guy working on a changeup," Palmer said.

"I am," Wilhelmsen said, transfixed.

"Well, I may not know much about pitching, but I did throw thirty-nine hundred and forty-eight innings and win 268 games," Palmer said, and started talking about changing speeds with his pitches.

Palmer was happy. And, for a while, so was Wilhelmsen.

Tony Phillips: A Short Man With A Big Chip

One late summer day in 1996, I was sitting with Mariners broadcaster Dave Niehaus in the visiting dugout of Chicago's U.S. Cellular Field when White Sox Tony Phillips began walking toward us.

Phillips was a 5-foot-9 infielder who's intensity was not just unnerving at times but could be over-the-top crazy. In a recent series in Seattle, he'd been ejected from two games.

"All of us short guys have a chip on our shoulder," Phillips had told me. "Competition just brings it to a head."

He was a man with many demons, not the least of which was crack cocaine. Phillips had been caught free-basing in a Southern California motel while playing for the Angels.

Now, a year later, he was with the White Sox– and before his career was over he would play for six teams – two of them twice. His team photos seemed staged, always featuring him with eyes abnormally wide. They did his mentality justice.

Niehaus was in his sixties when Phillips stormed into the dugout that day.

"Hey," he yelled. "I hear you said on the air that I needed anger management."

Niehaus shook his head. "No, after you were thrown out of the second game in that series, I said you were a candidate for anger management," he said.

Phillips stood silent for a moment.

"Well, hell," he said. "I can live with that."

Then he walked away.

Lou Piniella: Tough Guy With A Soft Heart

The only stories that made me laugh harder than Lou Piniella's were the stories told about him by everyone else.

Sam Perlozzo, Lou's third-base coach when they won a World Series together in Cincinnati, used to talk about Piniella's game management when the situation was tight.

"Most managers stay in one place during a game, so you know where to look for them in the dugout," Perlozzo said. "We got a hit and had a couple of guys on base and I look and Lou's not there.

"I'm starting to panic. Everybody's waiting for me to give the signs, and I can't find Lou in the dugout. Finally, I see him at the far end of the dugout. And he just waves at me."

Perlozzo shook his head.

"Then there were all the times we'd get a guy on first base and he'd start to give me signs and get impatient and just yell – 'Send him!' loud enough for everyone on the field to hear," Perlozzo said.

Then there was the Baltimore security guard, who called me aside one afternoon to tell me about Piniella had done the night before.

"He's walking back to the dugout after talking to his pitcher, and some fan gets all over him – and Piniella looks up, sees him and gives it right back," the guard said. "I mean, they're blistering each other and I'm thinking we're going to have an incident.

"This guy is 'M-F'ing Lou and Lou's 'M-F'ing him right back. Finally, Lou goes into the dugout and I ask him, 'You want that guy ejected?'

"And Lou looks at me and says, "No, no, the guy's fine."

Lou was a Damon Runyan character, the kind of man who had depth and doubts but was never compelled to put them on display. What you learned about Piniella came over time.

He was hired by the Seattle Mariners in 1993 to bring a franchise out of the woods. The Mariners had never been to the playoffs – had never even been close.

Ken Griffey Jr. told me about the first team meeting Piniella called in spring training.

"Lou walks around the clubhouse, telling us how he came here to win," Junior said. "He said he had no doubt the Seattle Mariners were going to turn the corner and win.

"Then he looks around the room and says, 'Of course, some of you won't be here.' *That* got everybody's attention."

By the time Piniella left Seattle, the team had been to the post-season, drawn three million fans in a season, and built a beautiful new ball park.

"I always hear that having Randy Johnson and Junior and Edgar Martinez saved baseball in Seattle," Jay Buhner told me. "We had those guys the year before Lou got here, and we lost almost 100 games. Lou taught us how to win.

"You want to talk about who saved baseball in Seattle, you'd better start with Lou."

A self-taught hitter as a player, Piniella played on the edge of rage, always angry at making outs, at opposing pitchers, at himself.

"His first season playing in Kansas City, he'd come back to the dugout, run up the tunnel toward the clubhouse and started screaming and throwing things," then-manager Bob Lemon said.

"Management came to me and said that tunnel was like a megaphone – everyone in the park could hear him.

"I banned him from the tunnel. Then I'd see him out in the outfield screaming at himself. I think fans bought seats out there just to listen to him."

Lou's first spring with Seattle, he tried to stay positive.

"I don't know how this team lost 98 games a year ago," he said.

A week later, the Mariners had lost six exhibition games in a row.

"I'm starting to wonder how this team won 64 games a year ago," Piniella said.

One year my daughter was learning to drive and, with me in the car, blew a tire out by going into a curb. I didn't want her losing confidence, so I made a tape for her in spring training.

I interviewed players and others about their first driving screwups and sent them to her. Piniella's was the funniest.

"Before I had my license, I borrowed the family car and went for a drive," he said. "I lost control, plowed through a fence and killed a cow. My father made me work on that farm all summer to pay off that cow."

Two years later, I met Piniella's mother, Margaret, and told her how Lou had helped my daughter. She was aghast.

"There was no cow!" she said. "And it was my fault. I left the keys in the car and ran into the house, and when I looked out, there was Lou backing down the driveway.

"He backed across the street and right through a fence, but there was no cow!"

As the years rolled on, I got to know Lou and he came to trust me. I visited him at home, and in spring training, we'd always have an off-the-record dinner or two.

During one of them, he talked about missing his family.

"When I played, I had a great time, played with wonderful teammates on good teams," he said. "Anita and the kids paid for that. Now, they live in Tampa and I'm here in Arizona for spring training, about to go to Seattle and manage.

"They're paying for that, too. You wonder how long you can do what you love to do at someone else's expense. You wonder if you can ever repay them."

Away from the ball park, Lou would talk about baseball – but try to stay away from it when possible. We talked about the stock markets and horse racing – he had a system for each – and about family.

One night at dinner, he surprised me by inviting two lovely young women at the bar to join us. I had seen enough men in the game head down this road, but never Piniella.

What Lou wanted, however, was simply non-baseball conversation – and he spent an evening asking our guests about their lives and ambitions. He never mentioned what he did for a living. He didn't ask for their telephone numbers.

When we left he smiled.

"Wasn't that a nice evening," he asked.

The Piniella I knew cared not just about those in baseball or his family, but about people in general. Of all the stories I was told about Lou, this one may be the most telling.

Piniella and good friend and coach Lee Elia were walking around a city after a loss, letting Piniella unwind on the road, when they encountered a woman on the street asking for money.

"She said she had a baby at home and had lost her job and her husband," Elia told me. "Lou said he wouldn't give her money but that he would help her."

They walked to a nearby grocery store and piled two shopping carts full of good food and baby supplies. Piniella then hailed a cab, gave the cabbie fare and had him drive the woman and her groceries home.

Sweet story, yes? Here's the most telling part.

"We're walking back to the hotel, and I'm thinking what a nice thing Lou had done, and I notice he's got tears running down his cheeks," Elia said. "He turns to me and asks, 'Did I do enough for her?'"

Bryan Price: When Failure Comes Knocking ...

Of all the character traits Bryan Price had to draw from, the one that served him best was this. When failure came knocking, he never answered the door.

Price had been in love twice in his life, once with a game, once with a woman.

After 16 years, that game tried to dump him. After five minutes, the woman wasn't certain she ever wanted to see him.

Neither happened.

Today, Price is married to the love of his life, Judy, and is a well-respected big league pitching coach with the ability to laugh at himself and most everything else.

His pitching career?

"I had a power mentality without a power arm," Price said. "I was destined to pitch in the big leagues. I believed that my whole life. I may have been the only one who believed it."

Meeting Judy for the first time?

"She was taking one for the team, talking to me so her friend could dance with my friend," he said. "I stared at my feet a lot."

Becoming a first-time minor league pitching coach?

"The Mariners said I could keep my minor league player's salary – but no benefits – if I wanted to coach their rookie league team in Arizona," Price said. "I said 'yes,' then started regurgitating everything anyone had ever told me about pitching."

Price could self-depreciate as well as anyone, but the more I talked to him, the more I saw a man absolutely dedicated to his craft – and to the men who were trying to do what he'd never been able to, get big league hitters out.

Spitting up things people had told him over the years – things that often hadn't worked and were only vague generalities – wasn't good enough for Price.

He studied mechanics and put to use the one advantage he had. He understood the mind of most pitchers, because he'd been one, scrambling to succeed.

"Pitchers are different animals," general manager Pat Gillick said. "Bryan gets inside their heads better than most anyone I've seen. You have to be able to get through to these guys. Bryan does."

A few months into his first big league coaching job, with Seattle, pitchers loved Price as a man and as their coach.

I asked veteran Norm Charlton about Price, he shook his head reverently.

"I spent a full spring training in Tampa Bay with Larry Rothschild, and he's supposed to be one of the best pitching coaches in the game," Charlton said. "He never said a word to me, and I got released.

"Bryan watched me throw two or three times and said, 'That won't work ...' and he was right."

At Price's suggestion, Charlton made a change in his delivery.

"He saved my career," Charlton said.

Then-rookie Joel Pineiro hit a stretch where he lost 3-to-4 miles off his fastball and got hammered. Between starts, Price suggested a change – and Pineiro's velocity jumped.

"My approach is direct. I'll make a suggestion based on what I know, what I see, and then they decide whether to try it," Price said. "I can't force them to do anything."

Price's mentor, grizzled manager Lou Piniella, laughed at that.

"Bryan works well with these young guys, he's only, what, 38-years-old?" Piniella said. "And you know what? He'll get right up in their faces when he has to.

"He knows pitching, he knows mechanics, he knows people. He may be the best I've ever worked with."

Over his five years in Seattle, I probably took a hundred photographs of Price, who was usually a delightful subject. He'd spot the camera and snap into a pose – The Thinker, one day, an angry guy flipping me not one but two fingers the next.

Always, there was a huge smile that followed. Price loved what he did, who he was, from the moment he awakened to the end of a long night at the ball park.

Lou Piniella left the team after 2002, and Price stayed on with manager Bob Melvin – getting Melvin to show a sense of humor he never wanted to share with the media.

After the 2004 season, Melvin was fired. Price was asked to stay on and did. Midway through the '05 season, my camera and I made a discovery.

Price wasn't smiling as much. In Kansas City, I asked him to lunch, told him what I was seeing and asked if it were true.

It was. Price didn't feel a part of the decision-making process with new manager Mike Hargrove and general manager Bill Bavasi. He didn't whine about it – never mentioned it until I got him at lunch.

Price said he was leaving at the end of the year, but asked me not to write it. That didn't please me, but I agreed – at least temporarily.

Price left and soon after joined Melvin with the Arizona Diamondbacks. When Melvin was fired, the team asked Price to stay on, but he didn't.

Loyalty, that kind of thing.

I telephoned and bet him he wouldn't be out of work more than a few months. He'd become too well known as a dynamic pitching coach to sit idle long.

Dusty Baker and the Cincinnati Reds came calling. The next spring, I took photos and Price couldn't stop smiling.

He and Judy had been married since '92 and were still head over heels for each other. Get Bryan away from the park, with a margarita in him, and he'd regale you with hilarious stories of his own pitching career.

Still, my favorite story came from a Class AA pitcher who never made the big leagues, one who Price worked with.

"One day a lot of guys threw bullpens, and the catcher who was supposed to catch me went into the training room for treatment," the kid said. "I thought I was done, but then Bryan put on the catching gear, got down behind the plate and said 'Let's go!' So I threw a bullpen to him."

It's how I picture Price. Without guile, a man with the gift of ideas, willing to do almost anything to help anyone in the game.

Kirby Puckett: From The Projects To Hall of Fame

The agony of toilet training – Randy Bush and his wife remember it well.

"We read books and manuals and talked to other parents, our doctor, everything," the Minnesota infielder said. "And Ryan wasn't buying any of it."

Finally, Bush had a major league idea. He put his 2-year-old son on the pot one more time, then told him: "Ryan, this is the way Kirby Puckett does it."

"That was it," Bush said. "Ryan was trained."

For parts of two decades in Minneapolis, everyone seemed to want to do things the way Puckett did them – and the Twins followed him to a pair of World Series titles.

Nearly as round as he was tall, Puckett was a 5-foot-8 package that major league scouts passed on out of high school and few pursued out of college. Puckett looked less like a center fielder than anyone playing the position.

What scouts missed initially was Puckett's tenacity and toughness. Raised in Chicago projects so troublesome even police wouldn't visit after dark, Puckett grew up on the 14th floor of a building without a working elevator. In his three-bedroom apartment, his parents had one room, three sisters shared another and the six Puckett brothers crammed themselves into the third.

Puckett played baseball – or some version of it – throughout his childhood. Using rolled up aluminum foil as a ball and a broomstick as a bat, Puckett formed his own league in an alley behind his complex.

At night, the Puckett brothers were entertained by Kirby's pitching. He threw rolled up socks.

He never lost that joy for playing the game or the perspective that it was just that.

At one point baseball's highest paid player, he entered the last year of a multi-year deal not in the game's top 35 but was never asked to renegotiate. And when Reggie Jackson used the Twins as an example of racism in a national interview – pointing out they were an almost all-white team built around one black player – Puckett just shrugged.

"My parents taught me never to pay attention to color," Puckett said. "People are people. These people happen to be my teammates – their color doesn't matter."

Puckett was a presence in the game, with teammates and opponents. Gracious with rookies, entertaining with the press, Puckett was the Twins, on and off the field.

"We all pass through this game, but Kirby will leave his mark," Tom Kelly said. "You won't find a guy in baseball he hasn't touched in some way."

It was Puckett's personality, his will to win, and his genuine affection for people that got him elected into the Hall of Fame after glaucoma forced an early retirement.

By the numbers, Puckett had a marvelous career that included a pair of World Series titles. By being himself, he became a smiling icon for athletes of his generation.

J.J. Putz: Merry Prankster With A Subtle Touch

Anyone who's spent any time around baseball players misses the goofy male camaraderie as much as the game itself when it's time to leave. And no matter how long a career lasts, the time to leave always comes too soon.

The humor is bawdy, often disgusting, and one of the hardest aspects of the game to translate to fans.

Think teammates Jay Buhner and Norm Charlton, wearing surgical gloves, delicately lifting an enormous turd from a toilet, placing it carefully on a plate and then proudly displaying it as a table setting.

It's not for everyone. It's not supposed to be.

J.J. Putz was a big man, a late-inning reliever during games and a merry prankster before and after them.

Sometimes he could be subtle. Pitcher Eddie Guardado was terrified of snakes, though he'd rarely encountered one. Putz told him he'd seen "a small one" crawling in Guardado's locker one morning.

Guardado was almost certain Putz was joking – but for a week he would reach in with a bent wire hanger to lift items in his cubicle.

One day in spring training I was watching some players taking early work on a field just after 7 a.m. and came across rookie reliever Mark Lowe running a lap – stark naked except for his shoes.

Turned out, Lowe had bet a teammate that the other player couldn't hit the foul pole with two baseballs in four tries.

Lowe lost, stripped down to his shoes and ran a lap in the nude.

It was just one of the things players do when they spent six weeks together every spring. I talked to Lowe, who thought it was funny, and to the general manager – double-checking to make sure a story wouldn't get Lowe in trouble.

It didn't. But Putz thought I'd crossed a line, putting something in the paper that should have stayed in the club-house. We talked it over and agreed to disagree. Sometimes it works that way.

Putz had been slowed that spring by a tender arm no one considered serious, but he hadn't thrown often in the bull-pen, so there was some concern.

Wandering between fields, I happened to walk by the bullpen area where Putz had just been throwing, under the watchful eye of manager Mike Hargrove.

I didn't know if J.J. was through or just beginning, so I stood against a chain link fence that surrounded the bullpen and waited to see. Putz turned his back to talk to Hargrove, who listened carefully – then threw a resin bag to the ground.

Putz didn't so much leave the bullpen as storm off, with me about five steps behind. I called to him but he kept moving, and I was thinking the news couldn't be good.

My pursuit went across a playing field, down a long hall-way and into the clubhouse, where Putz was leaning into his locker when I got there a few seconds behind him.

As I arrived, Putz faced me.

"Gotcha!" he said, and beamed, then punched me in the shoulder.

Not only had he seen me and set me up in the bullpen, he'd gotten Hargrove to go along with it. I laughed as hard as both of them – but my shoulder hurt for days.

Harold Reynolds: Ready To Talk Baseball

Harold Reynolds always seemed approachable, no small thing in a major league player. Articulate, full of energy and happy to be in the bigs, he was the perfect Seattle Mariner of the late-80s and early-90s – untouched by false pride.

On an east coast road trip, I'd filed my pregame notes when one of my editors, Paul Miller, asked a favor. His son, Joel, had lost a high school game earlier that day and was inconsolable – a pair of his errors had contributed to the loss.

"Could you ask Harold Reynolds what he'd say to a kid in that situation?" Miller asked.

After the Mariners game, after my post-game interviews, I passed the question on to Reynolds. Without a moment's thought, he asked how old Joel was – then asked for his home telephone number.

An hour later, from the team hotel, Reynolds called a young man in Washington he'd never met. The toughest part of the conversation was convincing Joel that he really was talking to Harold Reynolds.

Once past that, Reynolds talked about a championship game his team had lost in his senior year in high school – a game in which center fielder Reynolds had committed a pair of errors.

"When the game ended, I was in center field and I just sat down out there and started to cry," Reynolds said. "Next thing I know, I look up and my mom is standing there with me. I was like, 'Oh, mom!' It was bad enough we'd lost. Bad enough I was out there crying. Now I had my mom on the field with me."

Before he got off the telephone, Reynolds had Miller laughing – and looking forward to his next game.

When I talked to him the next day, I passed along the gratitude of a much-relieved father.

"Thanks," I told Reynolds.

"For what?" he said. "All we did was talk baseball."

Years after he'd retired as a player, his ability to talk baseball on television – with the same manner he'd done it with fans and teammates throughout his career – served him well at ESPN.

Reynolds' affection for the game and its fans is genuine. No small thing in a major league player.

Cal Ripken Jr: Just Get The Job Done

They tried to make a guy thing out of the longest consecutive games-played streak in major league history, but Cal Ripken Jr. wouldn't bite.

It wasn't because his father pushed too hard. It wasn't that Ripken wanted badly to show the old man what he could do.

The day he matched what was then baseball's longest streak – Hall of Famer Lou Gehrig's 2,130 consecutive games – I got to watch Ripken and talk to him.

His career was overshadowed by The Streak, and he knew it. Ripken had been 21-years-old when it began on May 30, 1982. He was 35 when he reached Gehrig.

"I love my job," he told me.

I gave him an 'oh, please' look. It couldn't be that simple.

"Every day, it's like being a little kid again," Ripken said. "It's a profession, and there are days you're not 100 percent, mentally or physically. But it's still baseball."

I telephoned his mother, Vi. She said Ripken had grown up – he was 6-foot-4 when he began playing for the Baltimore Orioles – but hadn't changed.

"He went to bed in his uniform the night before his first Little League game," she said. "I told him to take it off, and he did. When I went in later to make sure he was sleeping, he was wearing it again and had his glove in bed with him too.

"That's how much Cal loved baseball."

He learned that the sport was tough and that the men who

played it were tougher – and his best example came at home.

"I remember in the winter, my dad would play soccer and once he bruised his right big toe," Ripken said. "There was blood under the toenail. He came home, went out to the garage and got the drill. He drilled into the toenail, blood spurted out and he said 'aaaaaahhh!'"

That's tough.

Ripken played because he was among the most productive shortstops in the game, winning the Rookie of the Year award, then two American League Most Valuable Player awards.

Ripken played with a sprained ankle taped, on nights after he'd been hit in the head with a pitch, on swollen knees ...

"I never set out to break the record for consecutive games played. I just never got to the point where I thought taking the day off was the answer, and my managers kept putting me in the lineup," Ripken said. "For years I fought the notion that The Streak was my identity as a player.

"I played because it's what I do, and I never believed I would have helped my team by not playing."

On the day he tied Gehrig's record, Ripken hit a home run and had three hits. Afterward, in a post-game ceremony at Camden Yards, Ripken addressed a crowd of 48,804 who'd come to see history.

"I'm exhausted," he deadpanned. "I think I'll take a few weeks off."

It would be years before he didn't play, and when The Streak ended, Ripken had played 2,632 consecutive games. When Ripken retired after 21 seasons, he had 3,184 hits, 431 home runs and 1,695 RBI.

He was elected to the Hall of Fame in 2007.

"My dad's advice to us growing up was always simple. Whatever you took on, he'd say 'Just get the job done,'"

Ripken said. "That's what I tried to do.

"I'm a pretty good ball player, but I'm not in the category of Lou Gehrig. But one thing we shared, we both gave it our all, every day. We both showed up for work."

At the end of the 2011 season, only six big league players had active consecutive games streaks of more than 100 games.

"Two-six-three-two," Baltimore outfielder Adam Jones said, "is a number no one will ever approach. Guys who played this game can't believe someone did it. It's the most unbreakable record in sports."

Alex Rodriguez: Tightly Controlled Image

Alex Rodriguez came to the big leagues with an angel's face that made him appear an innocent. It's why men tell their daughters looks can be deceiving.

He arrived as a future Hall of Famer. That's what fans in Seattle believed, and A-Rod wanted to be the best that ever played. When he'd say that, he tried to sound as humble as Roy Hobbs, only driven.

There may not have been a more image-conscious player since Joe DiMaggio, who controlled how he was introduced at baseball events. When you interviewed Alex, he wanted to know why you asked certain questions, where you were going with your story.

It was a little disarming when he was 18. By the time he was 21, it had become downright disingenuous.

Alex would 'tip' you to milestones he was approaching, feed you anecdotes, like his 'close personal relationship' with the Yankee shortstop, Derek Jeter – which turned out to be an awkward surprise to Jeter.

Once in the Cleveland visiting clubhouse, Alex called me aside. The three traveling beat guys knew he worked a subtle rotation, and it was my turn to get a story,

Alex wanted me to know he was playing the Indians series despite being emotionally distraught – his maternal grand-mother had died.

"We were close, she meant the world to me," he said.

I got the details, and genuinely felt for Rodriguez, until I asked if he were going to attend her funeral.

"Oh, no," he said, as if it hadn't occurred to him.

He patted me on the shoulder and headed for the field and never showed a moment of sorrow. The next day, he asked if I'd used the story.

In that sense, Alex was like a child surprised to be caught by a parent. He was smart, but it never occurred to him that others were, too.

Without question, on a baseball field, he was better than almost anyone else. When dealing with the press, he often assumed he could manage what would be written about him by steering an interview.

Alex wanted to be seen as guileless but gifted, outspoken but respectful. He wanted men to see him as tough, women as sweet. In the clubhouse, teammates often shook their heads during his interviews.

"Just write that he's perfect," Jay Buhner once yelled as a writer talked to Alex.

During the 2000 season, Alex told me he was going to test free agency at the end of the year, on the understanding I could write it without attribution.

I did, and when the response was intense, he shrugged and said "there's no way a writer could know, because I haven't decided what I'll do. My focus is on playing for Seattle.'

Over the years that followed, Alex would talk to me where ever we encountered one another – Texas or New York – and seemed unfazed by the unpleasant revelations that had followed him. Steroid use in Texas. A long history with a New York call girl service and its madam. A messy divorce.

When we talked, more often than not, Alex drove the conversation down roads on which he was comfortable – like how proud he was when his hit total passed that of former teammate Edgar Martinez, or how overwhelmed he'd felt when he'd hit more home runs than Ken Griffey Jr.

"It's humbling," he'd say, and check to make sure I was writing that down.

And it probably would have been, to most. Just not to Alex Rodriguez.

Nolan Ryan: He Demanded Respect, Or Else ...

In Nolan Ryan's final spring with the California Angels, teammate Brian Downing was behind the plate when a Chicago Cubs rookie came to bat with a batting glove hanging out of each of his back pockets.

"Better tuck those in," Downing said. "Nolan doesn't like 'em."

"I don't care," the kid said.

Downing shrugged. Ryan's first pitch was a fastball that hit the rookie in the ribs and seemed almost to stick there. On his way to first base, the kid gingerly tried to tuck his batting gloves in.

Ryan was no one to trifle with on the mound, even in an exhibition game. Competitive, old-school and fearless, he spent a career dominating hitters. He won more than 300 games, lost more than 250 – and either way, he walked off the mound asking only one thing.

Respect.

Not just for himself, but for his team and, as importantly, for the game.

How competitive was Ryan? In the '70s, Ryan was with teams that never knew a pennant race. Against power hitters he respected – and was in turn respected by – Ryan would occasionally stand on the mound and mouth the word 'fastball' before the pitch.

He did it with Dick Allen. Reggie Jackson. A few others. He'd tell them what was coming and then both men would wait to see if it mattered. Usually, it didn't.

While with Houston later in his career, Ryan was charting pitches in the Astro dugout – preparing to start the next night's game – when Los Angeles rallied for a ninth-inning victory against Mike Scott.

Second baseman Steve Sax celebrated by carrying a teammate from home plate to the Dodgers dugout – and in the press box, veteran beat writer Gordon Verrell shook his head.

"Saxie must have forgotten who's pitching tomorrow," Verrell said.

Sure enough, Sax led off the next night – and Ryan's first pitch was at his head.

Message sent. Message received.

Ryan threw seven no-hitters and retired with 53 major league pitching records. Always, he respected the game. Always, he demanded opponents respect it, too.

Win or lose, but do it with class.

And if something he did angered you, Ryan was right there on the mound where everyone could find him. He was in his 40's when Robin Ventura charged him one night – and in film clips that still embarrass Ventura, Ryan is shown pounding the top of the batter's head with his right hand.

Ryne Sandberg: Just Wanted To Play The Game

Until the day he reported to Helena, Montana for rookie ball, Ryne Sandberg had never spent a night away from home. By the end of that first season, teammates and staff called him 'Gabby' because he rarely spoke.

Sandberg wasn't much of a third baseman, didn't hit for power, went about his work and disappeared.

And after 1981, when his major league debut consisted of six games, 13 at-bats and a single, there weren't just better prospects in baseball. There were better prospects in the Philadelphia system.

Shortstop Larry Bowa was traded that year from the Phillies to the Cubs, and when general manager Dallas Green asked him to suggest a good young player Chicago could ask for, Bowa told him Sandberg.

What was it Bowa saw that few others did?

"He did everything effortlessly," Bowa said. "He worked, but he never did any more than that."

What Bowa, Green and later manager Lee Elia wondered was how good the kid from Spokane could be if he worked relentlessly.

They found out.

A tireless worker whose life during the season was one continuous routine – repeated daily – he devoted himself to baseball. The result was Gold Glove defense at second base, a Most Valuable Player Award and the record for home runs at his position when he retired.

For all that, Sandberg was never comfortable talking. Not about baseball, not about life. Interviews were clipped, the answers pat. He was pleasant but not much help to a media trying to get his story.

After injuries on the field and marital problems off, Sandberg retired following the 1994 season, walking away too early at 35. Two years later, he made a comeback – too late at 37.

He never seized a microphone or a spotlight, never sought celebrity. Sandberg blushed when fans asked him to pose for photographs. Teammates adored him, but few knew him well.

"Really, I just want to play the game," he said once in spring training. "Everything else is what I put up with to do that."

Sandberg was one of the best ever to play his position, a mix of talent and late-developing work habits that created a Hall of Fame career.

Jeff Schaefer: Haunted By Anger At Father

Before any interview, you do all the research you can, and before the internet, that meant rooting through old clippings if you could find them, maybe talking to someone who knew the subject.

And sometimes, you get lucky.

Jeff Schaefer was a reserve infielder, a man who'd spent eight years in the minor leagues pursuing a chance at the big leagues. When he came to camp with the Seattle Mariners, the information in the media guide was sparse, but it had one nugget.

It said his father was a justice of the peace.

After I ran through the usual questions about on-the-field things, like a few brawls he'd been involved in, I asked about his father.

"That's my stepfather," Schaefer said, and his face changed, flushed. I stayed quiet, let him make a decision on whether to go on.

Jeff went on.

"In New York, my real dad was in what might be referred to as "organized" trouble. He took off, and I carry the anger for me and my mother and my sister – it's never gone away," he said.

"If my father walked in here this minute, I'd be torn between the Christian spirit of forgiveness and the nature of the streets, which would be to beat the crap out of him. It would be a toss-up."

A wild kid, he was gently moved toward athletics by the stepfather his mother married when Schaefer was 14. Justice Phil Rogers helped get him a baseball scholarship to the University of Maryland, and Schaefer signed with the Baltimore Orioles after graduation.

They assigned him to the Southern League.

"The last I'd heard, my father was down there somewhere," Schaefer said. "There were nights on the field I could feel him in the stands – nights I knew he was there."

Schaefer had a hair trigger. An inside pitch, a hard slide, an insult might set him off, and he'd be in the middle of the diamond, brawling.

"I wasn't always fighting the guys I was banging on," he said. "I didn't always realize it then, but I fought my father a million times out there. It was never calculated, I'd just snap.

"It was always him I was pounding once it started."

Schaefer pulled off his cap, showed me a photo he kept there of daughters Torey and Casey, and his eyes welled up.

"My kids got me past that," he said. "I wanted to be the father to them I didn't have. I carry my baggage and always will. I failed as a husband, but I will not fail as a father.

"I play in Seattle, they live with their mother in North Carolina. I talked to my ex-wife the other day and she said, 'You hung the moon in their eyes, and now you're not here to see it.'

"I call them. I talk to them. They know they have my unconditional love, but I'm a long way away."

Jeff Schaefer was all of 5-foot-10, a wiry, scrappy player I'd known little about when our interview began. With one what-the-hell question – one I'd had no reason to think would amount to more than a sentence in response – I'd gotten lucky.

Jeff's answers kept coming back to the same topic, and I

let him talk. His emotions were too raw to interrupt.

"I've grown up, but I may never get past my father," he said. "If I heard from him now, maybe I could forgive him, but I wouldn't want him to know me, to know my children.

"If I could say one thing to him, I guess it would be this. He did the best thing he could have done by getting out of our lives and letting my stepfather in. My mother is happy. My sister is happy. And I've got my girls and baseball.

"I'm trying to change my life," Schaefer said. "I'd like to be known as a father more than as a fighter. I want to be a good father. Maybe there's still time to be the man I want to be."

When I sat down to write the story, I used a stanza from a Bruce Springsteen song to set it up:

When I look at myself I don't see
The man I wanted to be
Somewhere along the line I slipped off track
Taking one step up and two steps back.

I have never heard the song since without thinking of Jeff Schaefer and hoping he found peace beyond a game he loved, with two daughters he adored.

And I've never forgotten the interview, where one out-of-the blue question turned it from a story on an anonymous middle infielder into the profile of a man in torment.

David Segui: Sense Of Fun Not Always Shared

David Segui gave me one of the funniest quotes I never used – the risk of talking to a genuinely funny guy while writing for a family newspaper.

It was the day after a clubhouse altercation between Segui and teammate Randy Johnson, who was going through one of his surly phases. Johnson asked Segui if he could change the clubhouse music and Segui said, "I don't care if you put on Barry Manilow."

That irked the Big Unit, who pushed Segui.

Wrong move.

Segui lifted Johnson off the ground and threw him into a cubicle–by which time teammates smothered both of them. Next day, Segui was sporting a heavily taped wrist that had been strained during the 'fight.'

I fed him a straight line. "What happened to your wrist?"

Segui shrugged. "I hurt it picking up a 6-foot-10 piece of shit," he said.

Didn't make the paper.

A second-generation player, Segui was a marvelous athlete at first base, quick and acrobatic with soft hands. Off the field, he was obsessed with fitness and perpetually carried around a small black doctor's bag.

Steroids? If so, Segui was too impatient to count only upon performance enhancers. He joined a 24-hour gym because he really did like working out during any of the 24 hours in a day. He asked me once to go with him – he wanted to put in a few miles on the treadmill. It was 2 a.m.

A single dad after a contentious divorce, Segui would spend much of spring training playing Mr. Mom to his son and daughter. He'd make them breakfast before coming to the ballpark, read to them at night. In between, he'd ride his Harley.

Segui was articulate and a good quote, who occasionally enraged one front office or another with criticisms they thought were cheap shots, but that he called honest.

He was something of an adventurer off the field, accepting changes far more readily than most in baseball. One day he went in for a haircut, for instance, and showed up at the ballpark blonde. And then there was his tongue ring ...

Segui's sense of fun was not universally shared in baseball, any more than his sense of style.

Having grown up in big league clubhouses following his father, Diego, Segui never viewed one as sacred. It was home, and at home Segui had fun.

Carlos Silva: Stirring The Poo

Following men under stress for months on end – and writing about them, through good stretches and bad – it's not as difficult as you'd think to irritate them.

Carlos Silva reminded me.

A big man, 6-foot-4 and 280 pounds, Silva had signed a lucrative multi-year free agent contract with Seattle, and then had the two worst seasons of his career in back-to-back years.

Near the end of his second season in Seattle, he'd spent much time on the disabled list, but made a few starts that didn't go well. One of them finished well after my deadline, so I hadn't had the chance to talk to him.

I got to the visiting clubhouse in Anaheim early on a Sunday morning, and Silva was at his locker. As always, when I approached a player, I didn't just start an interview.

My first question: Do you have a few minutes?

Silva said, "I don't want to talk."

I wasn't surprised. He'd worked hard and had little to show for it, his frustration on the field was reaching critical mass.

I talked to someone else for a notebook lead.

About 15 minutes later, another beat writer – Jim Street of MLB.com – entered the clubhouse, approached me and nodded toward Silva's locker.

"Carlos doesn't want to talk today," I said quietly.

Not quietly enough.

From across the clubhouse, Silva came toward us fuming.

"Why you got to talk about me, about my business?" he yelled, getting everyone's attention. "You don't know me!"

"I was only trying to save Jim time and you from having to talk to another writer ..."

"I know what you were doing. You were stirring the shit. You're always stirring up shit," he yelled.

And there, of course, was the great ethical debate of my profession. Is what I do giving the public access to players they want to know more about, or is it simply stirring up the poo and writing about it?

I believe the answer depends upon your perspective. I can understand why some people think the latter, especially when the story is about them,

In this case, however, I really hadn't been attempting to stir any poo.

I let it go. Trying to talk to Silva at that moment wasn't a wise option. Afterward, a player or two winked at me or shrugged. In the grand scheme of baseball confrontations, this hadn't even registered. It was just a thoroughly frustrated professional athlete blowing off steam.

I had a little fun with it – at my own expense as much as Silva's – with a blog that morning under the headline "Stirring up the poo ..."

A few days later, Silva approached me, whacked me on the shoulder with one huge meaty hand.

"We OK?" I asked him.

"Yeah, we're OK," he said.

Jim Slaton: Loved The Game, Loved His Brother

Everyone seemed to love Jim Slaton. Teammates gravitated to his competitiveness and humor. Women adored him. Opposing hitters couldn't even stay angry with him long.

Never a star, Slaton labored in obscurity with Milwaukee, Detroit, the Brewers again and then Anaheim in a career that spanned 16 seasons. In those years, he won 151 games, pitched 22 shutouts, and threw 86 complete games.

A competitor without an overpowering pitch, Slaton came back from a torn rotator cuff to pitch in and win a World Series game.

He loved the game, the clubhouse and life on the road. Slaton didn't gloat in victory, never blamed anyone for a loss. Unless he was on the mound, he was all smiles.

Always, he considered himself a shadow of his older brother, Frank, who'd played minor league baseball before he got so homesick he gave up the game, went home and took a factory job.

Slaton idolized his brother, spent most of his young life trying to match Frank's achievements.

Long after Slaton retired he'd become a minor league pitching coach for Oakland, Chicago, and then Seattle when Frank was diagnosed with cancer. Slaton called the Mariners and said he was sorry, but he couldn't coach that season. He wanted the time to be with Frank.

The Mariners held the job for him. Slaton spent months

living with his brother, taking him from one hospital to another, always looking for the treatment that might change the prognosis.

None came, and Frank Slaton died in his brother's arms. Slaton returned to the game they had shared all their lives, and rarely spent a day without silently talking to his brother.

Luis Sojo: Always A Major Leaguer

Luis Sojo was a Venezuelan infielder who played the game year round – springs and summers in the big leagues, falls and winters back home, where his family could watch.

Never fast, rarely a regular, Sojo played 13 seasons and got to the playoffs six times, to the World Series four.

I asked him once what he thought his greatest skill was.

"Being able to sit on the bench for days, then come in and do the job," Sojo said. "A lot of guys struggle with that job, it gets in their heads that they're not playing.

"I'm a major league player, whether I'm on the bench or in the game."

Richie Amaral played with Sojo and was amazed at his ability to make contact at the plate after not playing for days, sometimes weeks.

"When he's 50, he's going to be managing some winter ball team, put himself in to pinch-hit – and he's still going to make contact," Amaral said. "He doesn't care where a pitch is, he can hit it."

Sojo played a huge part in the Seattle Mariners '95 season, when they reached the post-season for the first time. It was Sojo's hit in a one-game playoff with the Angels that broke the game open.

A year later, he lost his job. The Mariners wanted to play rookie Alex Rodriguez. Sojo wasn't bothered a bit.

"Alex is like a bomb waiting to explode," Sojo said. "Me?

I'll play. I know what I can do."

Sojo's hit in that '95 playoff game is among the best moments in franchise history.

Seattle was leading, 1-0, when Sojo came to the plate in the seventh inning with the bases loaded against former teammate Mark Langston – once the Seattle ace.

"I don't swing if the ball bounces," Sojo said of his approach. "I remember telling myself that at-bat, 'OK, Luis, here's your chance to do something.'"

A right-handed hitter, Sojo lunged for a slider and grounded it sharply down the first base line. As the ball bounced around, two runs scored, and when the throw to the plate got away – and a third run scored – Sojo just kept running.

Langston wound up at home trying to cover the plate, but the throw to him was late. Sojo slid home safely and the game was Seattle's.

In a moment frozen in time, Langston lay on his back at home plate, beaten and frustrated. Sojo was on his feet, both arms clenched in front of him, screaming with pleasure.

"Some players don't like to show their emotions, but I do," Sojo said. "That whole season, the fans at the Kingdome had been so much a part of what we did, they deserved to share the excitement. I was emotional."

The following spring, I asked Sojo if he'd watched the video of that play often over the winter.

"I'm in Venezuela, and every few days someone would ask if I wanted to see that play again," Sojo said. "I'd tell them, 'Man, I got my own copy – what do you think?' I watched it a lot."

When Sojo retired, late in his 30's, he continued playing in Venezuela. When there was international completion, Sojo managed the Venezuelan team.

I ran into him before one of those games in 2009 and asked him if he could still make contact?

"Make contact?" he squawked in mock anger. "Man, I can still rake, what do you think?"

I think he was right.

Sammy Sosa: From Shoe Factory To Sports Hero

Any time Sammy Sosa needed a reminder of his childhood, he was no further away than the pile of shoes in his locker. Picking one up, Sosa can run his hand across the top and smile.

"This is what I did, I sewed these seams with a big machine in a factory at San Pedro de Marcoris," he said. "How can I not be happy playing baseball?"

That Puerto Rican city is known for producing major league players, including George Bell, Pedro Guerrero and Joaquin Andujar. None of them took longer to find the game than Sosa.

At 7, he was working in a shoe factory, bringing home what he made for the family. The first time he can remember buying something for himself was after he'd signed a professional contract.

Sosa didn't play baseball before he was 14. At 16, major league scouts began tracking him. By the time he turned 18, he was playing in the minor leagues in cities such as Gastonia, North Carolina, Sarasota, Florida, and Tulsa, Oklahoma, trying to learn both English and baseball.

By age 20, Sosa was a Texas Ranger. By 21, he was with the White Sox. By 23, he was a Cub. And no one was particularly impressed, except those back home.

"I go home every year, and every year I see that the shoe factory is still there," Sosa said. "Without baseball, I would still be there, too."

Over the years, Sosa became the pride of his country and one of the better power hitters in the history of a game filled with them. He found too many people who wanted something from him, too few without an agenda.

Somehow, Sosa got lost in the Spanish-to-English translation. When he had fun, he was portrayed as a player who wasn't bothered by losing. When he grew angry after losses, he was seen as moody.

He founded his own charity organization and began funding inner city baseball – in Puerto Rico and the U.S. – but the first time his foundation made headlines, it was when someone accused it of being a tax dodge.

On the brink of bitterness, Sosa was saved by the same thing that rescued him from that factory. Baseball.

During the '98 season, Mark McGwire staggered the game by hitting a then-record 70 home runs – and Sosa was right there with him throughout the summer, hitting 66. For months, the pursuit of Babe Ruth's record seemed to devour McGwire.

It brought the joy back to the game for Sosa.

For the first time, he was a national figure for what he was doing on the field. Those same smiles that had once earned him criticism now made Sosa a good-natured hero.

Thrust into the spotlight, Sosa responded with his best – on and off the field.

"Baseball is not prison, why wouldn't you love playing it," he asked. "I have never forgotten where I come from, where I would be without baseball. I thank God every day for baseball. Anyone in my situation would do the same."

Bill Swift: Born To Be A Baseball Player

The year Herb Swift turned 68, he didn't get out much. The years and 15 children had taken a lot out of him.

Not quite 30 years before, he was still pitching - $15 a game, and he'd give you both ends of a double-header too. He needed the money.

About the time Herb gave up sandlot ball, his 14th child was born.

"We'd run out of saints by then, so I wanted to name him after Ted Williams," Swift told me. "Named him William Charles Swift."

All his life, William went by Bill. And by his 23th birthday, Bill Swift was doing what his father had dreamed of almost every day of his life – pitching in the big leagues.

"I'm fulfilling his dreams and mine," Bill said.

The elder Swift made no bones about his influence on his sixth son.

"I sort of rolled a baseball to him on his blue baby blanket, and Billy sort of rolled it back," he said. "I used to say I threw a baseball into the crib with each of the kids, and Billy was the only one who threw it back.

"I left a baseball in his crib. It was his teething ring."

For all the schools and leagues Bill Swift played for growing up, the toughest competition came at the weekend family games, he said.

"There were nine girls, six boys and all the girls were tomboys," Bill said. "We'd have softball games and mom and dad would play, too. Mom would pitch, and we'd have somebody stand in front of her to protect her."

Herb Swift worked with his son on the fundamentals of the game, on pitching mechanics, and pitch selection. He wouldn't let him throw a curve ball until high school, remembering his own arm blowing out at about 39.

"I never had a fastball, just junk," Herb said of his own career. "I only weighed about 125 pounds – but I had a rubber arm!"

The family was from Portland, Maine, and poor. By Swift's fourth year in baseball, his salary – $375,000 – was more than his other 14 siblings earned, combined.

It gave Swift a sense of perspective and obligation.

"If somebody's car blows up, I help them get a new one," Swift said. "I bought my folks their house. I do what I can. They did it all for me."

Swift's career saw him pitch in relief and as a starter, and his toughness was never questioned.

In 1990, he was hit in the head by a line drive and the ball bounced into the stands on one hop. Swift argued to be allowed to finish the inning.

In 1991, Swift became the Mariners' closer and saved 17 games with a 1.99 earned run average. That December, he was traded to the San Francisco Giants.

A year later, in 1992, Bill Swift had the best year of his career, going 21-8 with a 2.82 earned run average and 233 innings pitched. It pushed him to a second-place finish for the National League Cy Young Award.

It was Herb Swift's last season. He taped each game he could find, and he and Bill would always talk the next morning. At 70, the Swift patriarch died.

Swift never had a season that matched '92, though he pitched 13 years, won 94 games, and appeared in 403.

When he retired, Bill Swift was named to Maine's Athletic Hall of Fame, and went into coaching – coaching his daughters in high school, then moving to Arizona and coaching a Scottsdale high school varsity.

He's in his 50s now, and still throwing batting practice.

Frank Thomas: They Called Him 'The Big Hurt'

They called Frank Thomas 'The Big Hurt' because of what he could do to a baseball at 6-foot-5 and 245 pounds.

The nickname fit, in part because of what Thomas did throughout a 19-year major league career, and to some degree because of the angst he felt over every slight.

There were quite a few and, if asked, he could rattle them off, even after he'd twice been named American League Most Valuable Player.

Back in high school in Columbus, Ga., he'd hit close to .500 and fielded about the same - a terrible defensive first baseman capable of hitting baseballs completely out of stadiums.

When they held the big league amateur draft in 1986, Thomas waited by the telephone. It never rang.

"I'd have signed for $5,000, that's how bad I want to play professionally," Thomas said. "Sixty-something rounds in that draft, nobody took me. Guys who weren't as good, guys I'd played against got drafted.

"I didn't. I went to my room and cried."

Signed years later out of Auburn, Thomas showed his potential by batting .500 in the spring of 1990. He didn't make the team and began the year in the minor leagues.

"I was raw, but I worked my butt off. I wasn't a blue-chip, can't-miss prospect, but I thought I'd earned a job," Thomas told me. "I went down and every time I hit a home run, drove in a run, I kept asking myself, 'They can't use this in the big leagues?'"

When he was called up that August, Thomas batted .331 and drove in 31 RBI in 60 games.

He never played a minor league game again - but he never forgot the time lost, either.

What Thomas was, at his size and with his power, was a hitter willing to take a walk, disciplined enough to lay off bad pitches and look for one he could drive.

"He's batting .377 and doesn't get any infield singles because he's slow," manager Lou Piniella said in 1994.

"There's never been a big man in the game like Thomas. He can launch on anybody and won't chase a pitch – he's probably on base half the damned time you face him."

That wasn't far wrong. In '94, en route to his second MVP award, his on-base percentage was .487.

Thomas was a force for the White Sox, producing at least 100 RBI in eight consecutive seasons. He was, at last, recognized as one of the best hitters in the game.

He was quick to smile, had a laugh that bordered on a giggle, and took teasing well. Posing for photos one day with Ken Griffey Jr., the photographer asked them to compare arms.

Junior immediately put his leg up against Thomas' forearm.

"That's about the same size," Griffey said, and Thomas giggled.

Still, the slights of the past bothered him. I asked him, in 1995, what could possibly still weigh on him.

"I didn't make the All-Star team in '91 or '92," he said.

As his career progressed, Thomas would greet me whenever we met and was always full of questions about Griffey Jr., whose prime coincided with his own.

"Pain motivates me," he said, "but Junior motivates me,

too. You want to be considered the best in the game? You know who you have to compare yourself with."

Griffey, of course, came up with a long-term plan for Thomas. Junior's son, Trey, was born just months ahead of Thomas' daughter.

"Frank, we've got to get them married and having kids – can you imagine the athletes we'd get? And by that time you and I can be their agents!"

"Let's do it," Thomas finally said. "Heck, let's get them married right now."

Thomas was never satisfied with his own performance, no matter how dominating. He wanted more.

"I've never understood how, when you ask good players, they say they don't think about getting to the Hall of Fame," Thomas said. "I want it, and I'm not embarrassed to say that.

"I want to be the best, not for a few years but for a long time. Junior is the same way – he always wants more."

After 16 seasons with the White Sox, Thomas was let go – just another piece of pain he took to heart. The next spring, I ran into him in an Oakland uniform.

"I'm not done," he said. "I'm going to prove it."

Then, he did.

For the Athletics in 2006, he played 137 games, hit 39 home runs and drove in 114.

When Thomas retired, he did so with a lifetime batting average of 301, 521 home runs and 1,704 RBI. He'll first be eligible for the Hall of Fame in 2013.

Thomas will be elected. If it's not unanimous, however, it's liable to bother him so much he'll come out of retirement and hurt something.

Andre Thornton: From Tragedy To Triumph

Andre Thornton was as genuine as the pain behind his eyes.

A solid player, Thornton swung a productive bat for the Cleveland Indians in the late '70s and early '80s. He was big and cheerful, and in a game that produced petty animosities, Thornton was everyone's friend.

In the winter of 1977, Thornton was driving from Ohio to Pennsylvania for a wedding, accompanied by his wife and two children. On an icy patch of road, their van spun out of control.

Gert Thornton and the couple's 3-year-old daughter died in the accident. Thornton and their 4-year-old son survived.

By the next spring, Thornton had arranged for Andy Jr. to accompany him on road trips. Grieving and suddenly a fulltime father, Thornton hit 33 home runs that year, had 105 RBI.

In nearly every city the Indians played, someone with a pad and pen or a TV camera or a microphone asked Thornton to talk about the accident.

A Christian, Thornton talked about his faith and that of his wife. Faith was all that got him through the days and nights since her death, he said.

One afternoon in Cleveland, I went to a television studio to watch Thornton tape an interview. Sincere and soft-spoken, he described a quiet drive through the snow, a moment of horror and then awakening, cold and in pain, to find half his family dead.

Thornton kept his composure throughout the interview, though tears ran down his cheeks. When he was finished, the TV crew huddled and the reporter turned to Thornton.

They'd had trouble with their camera. Could they do the interview again?

I have never known another man who would have said yes, but Thornton did. And when he talked about his wife and daughter a second time, the tears that appeared were honest and heartbreaking.

The woman behind the mike hugged Thornton when the interview ended.

Thornton played the game for another eight years. The sympathy others felt for him was never something he sought. The hugs – from peers, from fans, from members of the media – never stopped.

He received each with grace seldom found in or out of a clubhouse.

Steve Trout: Not Mystical, Just Sensitive

The day before I met Steve Trout, his pitching coach told me just how left-handed this left-handed pitcher was.

"The delightful thing about Steve is that he's unconscious out there on the mound," Billy Connors said. "He honest-to-God can't tell if he's pitching great or terrible, but he's the same guy either way.

"That's why I love him."

Over a 10-year career, the son of big league pitcher Paul Trout had pitched both great and terribly. His teams knew the difference, even if he didn't.

Trout won as many as 13 games in a season, lost as many as 16.

When he came to his first spring training with the Seattle Mariners, he brought a physical guru with him. They rose at dawn and walked out to the left field corner together.

Teammates had never seen anything like it.

"I need to know I'm putting in a little more, a little extra," Trout said of the stretching, hopping and bowing routines. "Negative feedback can interfere with talent."

One of 10 kids, he was the only one to follow his father into sports. With the Chicago White Sox, and then with the Chicago Cubs, he had a reputation for being a bit ... eccentric.

It's not hard to be seen as different in baseball, where almost everything one does is regimented.

"These workouts before the team workouts aren't mystical, and I don't want people thinking they're all I am," Trout said. "It works for me, but I'm sensitive about it."

Trout's first game with Seattle came in Oakland, and he pitched well until he got men on base. Then, runners rattled him. He threw one ball away, almost hitting himself in the foot.

"I have seen many things in my years," long-time manager Dick Williams said afterward. "I have never seen a bleeping pitcher throw a bleeping ball at his own bleeping foot."

Trout was goofy, no two ways about it. Everyone understood it but Trout.

Midway through the season, he approached me about writing a travel book with him – 'A Left-Handers Guide to Big League Cities.' I thought for a few moments, then asked if he planned on letting his personality show through.

"Absolutely," Trout said. "I've put a lot of things on tape, already."

I agreed to listen to the tapes, and he handed me about 20 mini-cassettes, each labeled with the name of a city.

At the team hotel that night, I put the first one on – Chicago – where he'd spent 9½ years – and waited for the thoughts of a left-handed mind.

"I'm a few blocks from Wrigley Field ..." Trout's voice said, then dropped the names of the cross streets, " ... and there's a Post Office here, if you needed to mail something ..."

I laughed, shook my head. Good one, I thought. Had me going. I pushed fast-forward, then play.

"If you're in downtown Chicago and need groceries, there's a little convenience store here about two blocks off the Miracle Mile ..."

I listened to hours of tape, it was all the same.

Steve Trout had walked around 'big league' cities with his tape recorder for days without making a single personal observation on where he was or what he felt about it.

He was 30-years-old and thought like an AAA map.

I told pitching coach Billy Connors about it, and he roared.

"I'll bet he thinks that'll be a best seller," Connors said. "Steve is hilarious, but he doesn't have a clue what's funny."

Mo Vaughn: Not A Fan Of The Press

Mo Vaughn read newspapers, which never made him doubt his talent. Occasionally, it made him wish he was illiterate.

"I was taught respect in school, I was taught to tell the truth," Vaughn said. "I don't understand the press, how it can make a good player out to be a bad guy. Do they want to hurt people? I don't understand it."

Touted as the next Red Sox superstar at age 20, Vaughn did what most young players do early in their careers. He struggled. And all that lavish press turned quickly.

"My family read in the papers that I couldn't hit, I couldn't play first base, I didn't belong in the major leagues and never would," Vaughn said. "I never forgot that."

So personally did Vaughn take those stories that after his first full year in the majors – when he hit 29 home runs and had 105 RBI – he was tempted to leave the game.

"I wanted to retire after that season. I almost did. The press made me so mad, a big part of me wanted to show them what I could do if given the chance," Vaughn said.

Friends and family talked Vaughn out of the thought, and the big man became an even better player. Even after winning the American League MVP award, Vaughn maintained humility. When I asked him if he'd like to play 162 games a season, Vaughn shook his head.

"I'm realistic," he replied. "I want to play 160 games a year – and miss the two games Randy Johnson starts against us."

Vaughn was a man who loved to hit and to laugh, and took pleasure in both. He was a star without pretense, who questioned the media's take on more than himself. When good friend Carlos Quintana was hurt, Vaughn never forgot how the story was treated.

"Carlos was written off, forgotten – it was like he'd never existed," Vaughn said. "That motivated me. Anger makes me play better. That's why I read newspapers."

A power hitter with subtle skills, Vaughn hit .300 or higher five times, hit .297 and .298 in two other seasons. And he reveled in trying to play the little man's game. In 1995 – a season shortened by a strike – Vaughn stole 11 bases in 15 attempts.

"Mo is making the rest of us first baseman look bad," Cecil Fielder joked.

That he played hard was never doubted, and extra effort was part of what cut short his career. Pursuing a pop fly into foul territory, Vaughn chased it into the visiting dugout in Anaheim Stadium. He lost most of a season because of that, and inactivity led to weight gain and a vicious cycle of debilitating injuries.

"The lessons of baseball apply to life. Every day you have to fight to keep your head above water, and every day you face failure," Vaughn said.

And when you fail?

Vaughn laughed. "You get to read all about it," he said.

Omar Vizquel: Gentle Man With G-Rated Humor

When a Cleveland comedy club invited Omar Vizquel to do a standup routine for charity, he accepted and wrote his own material.

"The other day in the dugout, my left foot fell asleep," Vizquel began. "I really hate that, because I was thinking 'Now it'll be up all night.'"

No, he never gave up his other job – playing shortstop as well as anyone ever has – but the joke was in perfect harmony with Vizquel's personality.

Rarely profane, in English or Spanish, the 5-foot-9 Vizquel was a gentle soul that young women found charming and older women wanted to adopt. His personality, like his sense of humor, was always 'G' rated.

On the field, he took delight in what his hands could do, and for years before games he entertained teammates and fans alike by playing catch the way he'd done it growing up in Venezuela.

As a thrown ball arrived, Vizquel would cross his hands in front of his body and – undetectably – deflect the ball from his closed glove into his bare throwing hand.

More than a few teammates trying to copy him caught baseballs with their chests.

The year Vizquel was a rookie, I tried to relearn the Spanish I'd taken long before in high school. The painful efforts delighted him. I introduced him to Mandarin Chinese food in Milwaukee and on the next road trip, he took me to a

South American restaurant where I tried to order 'albondigas.'

Every time we saw one another from then on, that was his greeting: "Albondigas!"

One year in Seattle he hosted a season-ending party for teammates who weren't surprised when Vizquel also invited members of the media and his own neighbors.

Vizquel saw everyone as a friend and treated them accordingly.

Larry Walker: OCD For The Number Three

Growing up in Canada, Larry Walker played hockey with an eye to the future – that is the few summer days when he and his friends could put together a game of baseball.

"We might play 10-12 games a year," Walker said. "It just wasn't played that much. No one gave a thought to playing baseball professionally."

There was a big league team in Canada no one took seriously, either – the Montreal Expos. What they saw in Walker was a Canadian athlete with the potential to play for a Canadian baseball team.

And they hoped that, with Walker's hockey dreams behind him – he'd been cut from two national teams – he might finally focus solely on baseball.

There were ... issues.

"I'd never seen anything but fastballs and what we called 'spinners,'" Walker said. "I never saw a changeup or a slider or a split-finger – nothing but fastballs. If it wasn't straight, I didn't even know what it was."

His first year in pro baseball, about all Walker did was hit the few fastballs he saw and swing and miss at everything else. Ken Brett, who managed a minor league team that Walker played for, loved the kid's heart.

"He was tough enough to fail and keep trying, which was great," Brett said. "Because he failed a lot."

Even Walker's father, Larry, had few expectations. "Everybody thought he'd be home soon," he said. "There just weren't any Canadian players in professional baseball."

After five minor league seasons, including one where he suffered an horrific knee injury in Mexico, Walker was called up to Montreal and, in 20 games, batted .170. A year later, he played 133 games and batted .241.

"Everything was new to him," a teammate said. "He'd ask you questions so basic you thought he was putting you on, but he didn't know the game. All his instincts were athletic, but he didn't know the game at all."

Walker learned, and along the way became something of a character.

His fixation on the No. 3 became an odd-if-charming quirk. Before stepping into the batters box, he would swing the bat to get loose – in multiples of three.

"I might need to swing six times if I felt tight," Walker said. "If I swung nine times, the umpires would tell me to get in the box."

He wore uniform No. 3, and would set his alarm to the nearest set of threes possible. Teammates never tired of asking him to talk about his family, then roared with laughter when he'd tell them about his parents, Larry and Mary, and his brothers – Gary, Cary and Barry.

"I got married at 3:33 p.m., "Walker told me. "And I was divorced three years later."

He had speed, a great arm, superb hand-eye coordination. When he managed to put it together, Walker became a star. From 1997 though 2001, Walker batted .350 or better four times, averaged 31 home runs – despite missing half a season to injury – and drove in 486 runs.

Walker was the National League's Most Valuable Player in '97, when he hit .366 with 49 home runs and 130 RBI.

"I love the game and the people in it and owe them a lot," Walker said. "I've been through injuries and a divorce, things most fans don't care about – and why should they?

"I never wanted someone in my clubhouse or in the stands to wonder what was going on with me that day. So I smiled a lot and did my job."

When Walker retired after 17 seasons, he'd been an All-Star five times, a Gold Glove winner seven times, and had forged a .313 career batting average.

He was enshrined in the Canadian Sports Hall of Fame. And when he went home in 2006, the young athletes of his country had embraced baseball – entire leagues had sprung up in part because of Larry Walker's success.

Tom Wilhelmsen: Baseball or Dope? Baseball

At 19, Tom Wilhelmsen faced a life-changing decision – continue his career as a highly rated minor league prospect or keep smoking dope.

For Wilhelmsen the choice was clear.

He walked away from baseball, became a bartender and traveled the world, smoking as he went.

A 6-foot-6 free spirit, Wilhelmsen was playing co-ed, beer-league softball with his girlfriend in 2008, when he reconsidered life and baseball, drove to his father's house and asked a question.

"Do you want to play catch?"

Three years later, Wilhelmsen was in the big leagues, throwing 98 mph and winning a job in the Seattle Mariners bullpen.

Yeah, Wilhelmsen was a fun interview.

"I wasn't ready to be a professional when I came out of college," he said. "My heart wasn't in baseball. I wasn't dedicated, I wasn't preparing to pitch.

Drug tests detected marijuana in his blood system. Twice.

The Milwaukee Brewers gave Wilhelmsen a strict warning after his first infraction. When he tested positive again, they gave him an ultimatum.

"When I got caught the second time, they sent me to rehab, and to make sure I took it seriously, they wanted me to pay for it – something like $28,000" Wilhelmsen said.

"It didn't work. If I wanted to play baseball, I had to do a lot of things differently, starting with not smoking grass. I was in rehab with meth addicts, heroin addicts. I didn't think I belonged there, so I left."

Wilhelmsen walked away from baseball, and stayed away for five years.

"I wanted to experience life my way," Wilhelmsen said, "so I did. I saw the world and fell in love. I traveled. I smoked. I had a great time."

He would tend bar in a Tucson nightspot, save money for his trips and then disappear. Wilhelmsen and fiancé Cassie made a tour of National Parks then moved on to Europe.

Wilhelmsen became a collector of sorts. He kept sand, taken from every beach and desert he visited, keeping them in small vials.

One day, playing outfield while Cassie played second base in a beer-league game, he began to consider the responsibilities of his life as a potential husband, a potential father.

"I didn't want to tend bar the rest of my life, come home every night at three or four in the morning," he said. "I thought I'd give baseball another try. I drove to my dad's, and started throwing again."

It was Fathers Day, 2008.

The comeback wasn't mercurial.

"I started by playing in a men's league with a couple of friends, then I heard about an Independent League team starting in Tucson and sent them an e-mail asking for a tryout," Wilhelmsen said.

"They called back during my wedding reception."

After his and Cassie's honeymoon, Wilhelmsen tried out and made the team.

The next year, Wilhelmsen's agent called the Mariners general manager, Jack Zduriencik, in part because Zduriencik had been with the Brewers when Wilhelmsen was first drafted.

Zduriencik remembered Wilhelmsen.

"His arm was special," Zduriencik said. "Really special."

The Mariners watched Wilhelmsen throw and offered him a minor league contract, which he signed. In 2010, he pitched for three teams in the Mainers minor league system.

In 2011, he was invited to spring training.

"I think I have, maybe, a 2 percent chance of making the team," he told me on the second day of camp. "I'm going to enjoy every moment I'm here, work hard and learn."

And dope?

"When I decided to try and come back, I gave up smoking entirely," he said. "I love the game again."

Wilhelmsen made the team.

As the season began, he thought he might begin collecting dirt from each big league mound he pitched on, add to that collection of sand.

"Cassie said 'no,'" Wilhelmsen admitted. "She said 'There's a fine line between collecting and hoarding.'"

Wilhelmsen struggled with his command and wasn't pitching much when the Mariners sent him to the minor leagues that summer. He pitched well and returned later in the summer, and success followed him.

What had he found in the minor leagues?

"The strike zone," he deadpanned.

By the end of his first year in the big leagues, Wilhelmsen had become an eighth-inning specialist, the setup reliever in games Seattle led.

When the season ended, he headed back to Tucson with Cassie. Might he pull a few bartending shifts at his old job?

"I might," he said. "I loved the people there and it's a pretty cool place."

Dick Williams: Hated Writers, But Needed Them

By the end of a marvelous managerial career, Dick Williams had outlasted his time and knew it.

A man whose career began when managers ruled their clubhouses, he pushed three franchises into the post-season, won a pair of World Championships and 1,571 regular-season games.

By 1988, Williams was managing in Seattle. A man with considerable pride in his accomplishments, Williams began losing interest early in one-sided Mariners games.

Like an indignant grandfather, he railed at the spoiled players he saw in today's game. The real men of baseball had played in his day. Now, it was all about the money.

As with everything he said, Dick Williams had a point – he was simply too unforgiving to win many allies.

Cross the Williams line and you simply ceased to exist in his world. That included players, coaches, owners and writers. As that line kept moving, that group kept growing.

Somewhere in their time together in San Diego, Steve Garvey had crossed the line. It may have been Garvey's squeaky-clean image – which was just that, an image. It may have been the attention the fans paid to Garvey instead of Williams.

Whatever the case, when asked about the great players he'd managed, Williams had wonderful stories to tell about Carl Yazstremski and Catfish Hunter, Rollie Fingers and Reggie Jackson, Jim Lonborg and Tony Gwynn.

When Garvey's name was mentioned, Williams shook his head.

"I have no recollection of Steve Garvey," he said. And that was the end of that discussion.

Williams enjoyed talking to the media, as long as it was on his terms. Talk to players if you must, speak to coaches if you wanted to – just make sure the final word belonged to the skipper.

Early in my first spring covering Seattle, I was one of three writers in camp. Somehow, we crossed that Williams line, and he informed us he was no longer speaking to the media.

The other two writers were Williams veterans, Jim Street and Bob Finnigan. Their suggestion: boycott the manager.

Next afternoon following the workout, all three of us gathered around pitching coach Billy Connors, a funny, charming fellow who loved, and was loved by, players.

Williams stared at us from the dugout, and then disappeared. Finished with Connors, I sought out players in the clubhouse.

As I passed the manager's office, Williams emerged, seemed to spy me for the first time all day and threw a friendly arm around my shoulders.

"Anything you need today?" he asked.

Turns out, the one thing Williams hated more than the press was being ignored by it.

Dick Williams ran his life and career his way, which made his bitterness after the fact all the more poignant.

Dan Wilson: Didn't Like To Talk About Himself

Nothing legal could make Dan Wilson talk about himself.

A catcher for the Seattle Mariners in the years when the team had stars like Ken Griffey Jr., Randy Johnson, Alex Rodriguez and Edgar Martinez, Wilson was happiest when he could catch a good game and head home to his wife and family.

Media interviews? When they were requested — which wasn't often — Wilson made himself among the more boring quotes in baseball. It was intentional.

"He's a solid guy with a sense of humor that, like most men's, isn't quite as good as he thinks it is," said his wife, Anne. "He's honest. He loves children. Dan is the kind of man that married women and kids love."

Wilson grimaced at that — not exactly what a manly man wants to hear of his image. But Wilson's grit was never questioned by his teammates.

Catching 98 mph fastballs from Randy Johnson, he'd have to ice his hand after each game. Norm Charlton fork balls? Freddy Garcia's sinker? Wilson wouldn't say a word, even to his wife, when he hurt.

"He'd come, get into bed and I'd see the new bruises," said Anne, who met her future husband when both were in the third grade. "The only time I'll know he's hurting is when he gets out of bed in the morning and groans a little."

Wilson could always handle pitching and pitchers when he was behind the plate, although he had far more trouble early in his career at the plate. Hitting coach Lee Elia became family — "Uncle Lee" — and Wilson's hitting improved so much that in 1996 he made the All-Star game.

The next year, the team gave fans a commemorative poster of the five Seattle All-Stars and Wilson, who didn't have a trophy case in his home, had it framed.

"I couldn't believe I was on a poster with Junior and Alex and Edgar and Jay (Buhner)," Wilson said.

He was the big league player as everyman, a guy who bought a home in a regular neighborhood in part because 'it had a lot of kids in it.'

The Wilsons adopted a Bulgarian orphan, Sofia. They each worked at a Northwest school for homeless children — and Wilson got a local company to kick in a donation to that school for every base runner he threw out.

"That's a lot of pressure," he deadpanned. "I've got to make budget."

How much did Wilson love his job? When the 2005 season began, he announced it would be his last. On May 4, he tore his right anterior cruciate ligament.

That appeared to be that.

Except Wilson, 36, decided he didn't want that injury to be anyone's last memory of him in baseball. Though doctors patiently explained the timetable for recovery was often eight months, Wilson went to work.

"Dan could have made it easy on himself and just done the usual rehab into the off-season," team trainer Rick Griffin said. "Instead, he busted his butt every day for four months hoping for one last game."

On Sept. 30, the Mariners stunned their fans by posting a lineup that had Wilson catching. His knee would allow him to crouch, to throw, but not yet to swing a bat.

When Jamie Moyer trotted to the mound to warm up before the first inning – and Wilson hunkered down behind the plate to catch him — Safeco Field erupted in a long ovation.

Wilson caught one inning, and then moved into retirement.

Quietly, of course.

Tiger Woods: Dropping By For Batting Practice

There may be no more cynical group in America than the players in a major league clubhouse when it comes to star worship. Unless a star appears.

Players sign autographs often but without great enthusiasm and seem genuinely mystified about their status among other mortals. But let a Hollywood celebrity like Kevin Costner show up in a clubhouse and watch the scramble.

Baseballs, bats, posters hurriedly purchased by bat boys all magically appear and are offered up for signature by beaming players.

Still, it's rare that anyone walks into a big league club-house and awes those who work there. Tiger Woods was an exception.

Neighbor, friend and occasional playing partner of Ken Griffey Jr., Woods had a standing invitation to take batting practice with the Mariners, but for years the scheduling never worked. When it did, during a Seattle visit to Minnesota, Woods arrived without entourage, quiet and almost shy.

Bedlam ruled. The equipment manager suited Woods out in full uniform. One of the Mariners coaches took off his game jersey and asked Tiger to sign it. Manager Lou Piniella wanted to talk putting.

On the field, Woods turned his cap backward ala Griffey and stood in the batting cage with a borrowed bat, a pair of batting gloves and great intensity. But the man whose towering drives inspire awe couldn't get a baseball in the air. Tiger made contact – sometimes solid contact – with virtually every pitch, but wore an AstroTurf path with his ground balls.

Mariners and Twins players surrounded the cage, shouting encouragement. Woods swung again and again, producing grounder after grounder.

"Golf balls don't move," Woods said, laughing.

Piniella wasn't fooled.

"Give him one week and with that hand-eye coordination he'd be hitting line drives," Piniella said.

Players and coaches from both teams wanted their pictures taken with Woods, who seemed to warm to the requests.

"Golfers all want to be ball players, ball players all think they're golfers," Woods said, laughing. "But there's a reason you don't see two-sport stars."

To Find Out More

Find out more about the players and managers in this book at these websites:

http://mlb.mlb.com/index.jsp

http://espn.go.com/mlb/

http://msn.foxsports.com/mlb

http://aol.sportingnews.com/mlb

http://bleacherreport.com/mlb

http://www.mlbdailydish.com/

http://blog.thenewstribune.com/mariners/